T0318709

Cambridge Elements ≡

Elements in Criminology
edited by
David Weisburd
*Department of Criminology, Law and Society, George Mason University; Institute
of Criminology, Faculty of Law, The Hebrew University of Jerusalem*

DEVELOPMENTAL CRIMINOLOGY AND THE CRIME DECLINE

*A Comparative Analysis of the
Criminal Careers of Two New South
Wales Birth Cohorts*

Jason L. Payne
Australian National University

Alex R. Piquero
University of Miami and Monash University

CAMBRIDGE
UNIVERSITY PRESS

CAMBRIDGE
UNIVERSITY PRESS

University Printing House, Cambridge CB2 8BS, United Kingdom

One Liberty Plaza, 20th Floor, New York, NY 10006, USA

477 Williamstown Road, Port Melbourne, VIC 3207, Australia

314–321, 3rd Floor, Plot 3, Splendor Forum, Jasola District Centre,
New Delhi – 110025, India

79 Anson Road, #06–04/06, Singapore 079906

Cambridge University Press is part of the University of Cambridge.

It furthers the University's mission by disseminating knowledge in the pursuit of
education, learning, and research at the highest international levels of excellence.

www.cambridge.org
Information on this title: www.cambridge.org/9781108794794
DOI: 10.1017/9781108882149

© Jason L. Payne and Alex R. Piquero 2020

First published 2020

A catalogue record for this publication is available from the British Library.

ISBN 978-1-108-79479-4 Paperback
ISSN 2633-3341 (online)
ISSN 2633-3333 (print)

Developmental Criminology and the Crime Decline

A Comparative Analysis of the Criminal Careers of Two New South Wales Birth Cohorts

Elements in Criminology

DOI: 10.1017/9781108882149
First published online: September 2020

Jason L. Payne
Australian National University

Alex R. Piquero
University of Miami and Monash University

Author for correspondence: Jason L. Payne, jason.payne@anu.edu.au

Abstract: Throughout the 1990s, many countries around the world experienced the beginnings of what would later become the most significant and protracted decline in crime ever recorded. Although not a universal experience, the so-called international crime-drop was an unpredicted and unprecedented event that now offers fertile ground for reflection on many of criminology's key theories and debates. Through the lens of developmental and life-course criminology, this Element compares the criminal offending trajectories of two Australian birth cohorts born ten years apart in 1984 and 1994. We find that the crime-drop was unlikely the result of any significant change in the prevalence or persistence of early onset and chronic offending, but the disproportionate disappearance of their low-rate, adolescent-onset peers. Despite decades of research that has prioritized interventions for minimizing chronic offending, it seems our greatest global crime prevention achievement to date was in reducing the prevalence of criminal offending in the general population.

Keywords: crime-drop, birth cohort, life-course criminology, developmental criminology, criminal careers, onset, chronicity, offending trajectories

ISBNs: 9781108794794 (PB), 9781108882149 (OC)
ISSNs: 2633-3341 (online), 2633-3333 (print)

Contents

1 Introduction

For almost two decades and in almost all corners of the western world, criminologists have observed a significant and sustained downward trend in crime. These declines have been documented from North America (Blumstein & Wallman, 2000; Zimring, 2007; Ouimet 2002), to the Asia-Pacific region (Mayhew, 2012; Weatherburn & Holmes, 2013), and in much of Western Europe (Aebi & Linde, 2010). Although the timing and magnitude of this so-called "crime-drop" has varied from country to country, one feature has emerged as internationally consistent. Specifically, the decline in aggregate crime rates has been most evident in youth populations (Andersen et al., 2016; Backman et al., 2014; Blumstein, 2006; Cook & Laub, 2002; Farrell et al., 2015; Kim et al., 2015; Morgan, 2014; Soothill et al., 2008; Von Hofer, 2014), so much so that contemporary analyses of the crime-drop have sought to rename the phenomena as the "youth crime-drop" to better convey the true nature of the decline and to focus researchers on its most likely causes (Matthews & Minton, 2018, p. 300).

In Australia, the crime-drop has also been a significant feature of the criminal justice landscape since 2001 (Weatherburn & Holmes, 2013) and has been the subject of multiple investigations. These studies have been almost exclusively conducted in the country's most populous state, New South Wales (NSW), where there has been a 50 percent drop in the rate of theft and a 33 percent drop in the rate of robbery. This, according to Clancey and Lulham (2014), has consequently produced a saving of $5.15 billion to the NSW community (as of 2014). Like elsewhere, the NSW crime-drop has been driven mainly by substantial declines in youth crime across most categories of offending (Hua et al., 2006; Payne et al., 2018).

Efforts to understand the crime-drop have focused almost entirely on changes to the aggregate crime rate, often presented as cross-sectional population standardized rates of offending by age (see Matthews & Minton, 2018). Essentially, this type of analysis seeks to quantify and interpret year-on-year changes to the age-crime curve and, in its most sophisticated form, attempts to parse out both period and cohort effects for their independent but complementary explanatory value. In the most recent study of this kind, Matthews and Minton (2018) examined the crime-drop using a visual analysis of shaded contour plots to compare changes in annual age crime curves generated from Scottish conviction data between 1989 and 2011. Their analysis compares the age-crime curves generated from twenty-two cross-sectional snapshots and the contour plots provide valuable insight into both period and cohort effects. Their data confirm that the Scottish crime-drop was similarly a youth phenomenon that started first with a decline in property crime throughout the 1990s and was followed by substantial declines among other crime types in the late 2000s.

Although the empirical efforts of Matthews and Minton (2018) represent one of the largest cross-sectional studies of age-crime curves in the context of the crime-drop, their analysis is nonetheless limited by its cross-sectional design. In a state-of-the-art review on age-crime curve research, Loeber and Farrington (2014, p.13) caution against a reliance on macro-level cross-sectional comparisons because such efforts risk "confounding the influence of multiple cohorts" and obscuring the potentially important developmental differences that underlie changes in individual and population level offending (see also Berg et al., 2016; Jennings et al., 2016). It is here that the current study makes a novel contribution to the empirical analysis of the international crime-drop phenomenon.

Specifically, instead of comparing annual cross-sectional age-crime curves, as has been the case in the bulk of crime-drop research to date, we present a unique comparative analysis of cohort-level and individual-level longitudinal development using two Australian (NSW-born) birth cohorts – cohorts that-straddle, developmentally, the commencement of the NSW crime-drop in the year 2000. Our cohorts were born ten years apart. The first, born in 1984, experienced their entire adolescence (ten to seventeen years of age) at a time when crime in NSW was persistently increasing. The second cohort, born in 1994, traversed their adolescence at a time when crime in NSW was in rapid decline. This later cohort of young boys and girls turned ten years of age (the age of criminal responsibility in NSW, and the age at which formal crime records are first kept) three years after the crime-drop began. Although relatively rare, comparative birth cohort analyses of this kind have been instrumental in criminology (see Fabio et al., 2006; Farrington & Maughan, 1999; Tracy et al., 1990), especially in exploring some of the discipline's most contentious issues regarding the coexistence of stability and change over the life course (e.g., Jennings et al., 2016). In this analysis, we exploit the fact that our two cohorts are from developmentally distinct periods (pre and post crime-drop), which not only adds value to the landscape of existing birth-cohort analyses, but provides for an internationally unique insight into the possible developmental causes and consequences of this international phenomenon.

Consistent with the growing body of crime-drop research, our analyses presented herein show a significant fall in crime. Our youngest cohort was responsible for almost 50 percent fewer offenses than their peers born ten years earlier. Contrary to our expectations, however, this decline was disproportionally the result of the less crime committed by low-rate or adolescent-limited offenders and almost no change in the population prevalence or long-term offending trajectories of those offenders we have traditionally described as early onset. Whatever caused the crime-drop seems not to have affected all offenders (or potential offenders) equally and this differential experience across the population provides fertile ground for theoretical and empirical reflection. In our view, the results suggest that the crime-drop was not the result of some purposeful effort to reduce the offending of frequent offenders (as has become a criminological mantra since Wolfgang and his colleagues (1972) identified the chronic recidivists in the first Philadelphia Birth Cohort study), but a wider social transformation that likely has restructured criminal opportunities making crime (relative to other activities) less likely. We see this result not as a rejection of the need for comprehensive interventions for high-risk youth, but as a promising reminder that crime-reduction strategies should not ignore the much larger number of less serious offenders whose crime may be more easily prevented and at lower cost.

The international "crime-drop"

It is difficult to pinpoint when and where the crime-drop was first identified and reported, largely because in the earliest phases some jurisdictional government reports of official crime statistics had documented the change in trend, but stopped short of naming it an official "drop" or "decline." In those early years, there was little reason to believe that the drop was any more than a statistical aberration. Criminologists now know that the crime-drop started in both the United States and Western Europe during the late 1980s and early 1990s (Blumstein, 2006; van Dijk & Tseloni, 2012), although the estimated starting point of the drop varied by jurisdiction and depended on the data source. In a seminal review, Blumstein (2006) showed that for the United States, the national decline in officially recorded murder and robbery offenses started in 1993 and persisted in a year-on-year decline until 2000.[1] By this time, both robbery and murder had fallen by 40 percent and have since plateaued at these historical lows. In Canada (see Farrell & Brantingham, 2013; Hodgkinson et al., 2016; Mishra & Lalumière, 2009; Ouimet, 1999, 2002), the experience was mostly consistent with the United States, although the drop in homicide, for example, appears to have started and plateaued a year or two earlier, while the magnitude of the decline was not as large (Mishra & Lalumière, 2009).

Across the Atlantic, the crime-drop in Western Europe also began in the early to-mid 1990s (van Dijk & Tseloni, 2012). Like in the United States, Scottish data suggest that the drop also started in 1993, but only if the measure of crime

---

[1] Van Dijk and Tseloni (2012) alternatively used self-reported victimization data from the International Crime Victimization Survey (ICVS). They show that the crime-drop in the United States is actually likely to have commenced somewhere between the 1988 and 1992 IVCS surveys.

uses the total quantum of official convictions for all offense types (Matthews & Minton, 2018). The actual number of convicted individuals was declining from as early as 1989, although the limits of the Scottish conviction data prohibit a more thorough and longer-term historical analysis. In an earlier study combining Scottish data with police statistics and self-reported victimization data from fourteen other Western European countries, Abei and Linde (2012) provide one of the most comprehensive regional studies of the crime-drop to date. Their analysis explores disaggregated crime trends in theft, burglary, and motor vehicle theft, as well as assault, robbery, homicide, and drug offenses. They conclude that in the combined experience of these Western European countries, the crime-drop was almost exclusively a property-crime phenomenon that commenced in 1992 and continued through to the end of the available data series in 2007. This was a shared experience for all three property-crime types, although the rate (and functional form) of the decline varied. Domestic burglary, for example, fell more quickly than either theft or motor vehicle theft in the mid-1990s, even though the overall decline (to 2007) in domestic burglary was not as great as it was for motor vehicle theft. By contrast, violent and drug crimes did not decline in Western Europe over the same period. Unlike in the United States, recorded assault rates and self-reported assault victimization increased from 1990 to 2007. For robbery, official rates remained unchanged between 1990 and 1998, then increased briefly through to 2002, only to return to the same levels seen in the mid-1990s. Self-reported robbery victimization data also evidenced an increase over the same period. The only exception was the recorded rate of homicide, which began to decline in 1993. Elsewhere in Europe, property crime was also in decline after the year 2000, according to results of the International Crime Victimization Survey (ICVS,) from former Communist countries of Estonia, Poland, and Georgia (van Dijk & Tseloni 2012).

In the Asia-Pacific region, crime statistics and victimization surveys have also evidenced a decline in crime in Australia (BOCSAR 2019), New Zealand (Mayhew, 2012), as well as Japan, Taiwan, and Hong Kong (Sidebottom et al., 2018).[2] In both Japan and Taiwan, the crime-drop appears to have commenced in the mid-2000s, some ten years later than in North America and Europe (Sidebottom et al., 2018), while in Hong Kong the crime-drop has been substantial in size, but internationally anomalous insofar as the decline appears to have started earlier than elsewhere in the world, sometime between 1980 (motor vehicle theft) and 1985 (burglary). In Australia, crime-drop studies have been

---

[2] As part of the United Nations Survey on Crime Trends and Operations of Criminal Justice Systems, del Frate and Mugellini (2012) noted a decline in homicide rates in other East and South-East Asian countries such as Singapore, Bhutan, China, Myanmar, Cambodia, India, Thailand, and the Philippines.

limited to the analysis of crime rates in NSW, the country's most populous state and the site of the present study. In that state, the decline in robbery and other property crimes commenced in the early months of the year 2000 and have continued, largely unabated, through to even the most recent available data from 2018. Property offenses[3], for example, peaked in late 2000 at 650 incidents per 100,000 persons. By the end of 2017, the statewide property offense rate was approximately 60 percent lower at 230 incidents per 100,000 persons. Violent crime[4] has also declined in NSW, although the downward shift started later (in 2003) and the decline has not been as large (currently 85 incidents per 100,000, down 30 percent from its peak).

The Local "Crime-Drop'

The now considerable wealth of collective empirical evidence shows that the crime-drop has been an international phenomenon, experienced mostly, although not exclusively, by high-income industrialized countries from all corners of the globe. So widespread is the experience of the crime-drop that Farrell et al. (2014, p. 421) described it as the "most important criminological phenomenon of modern times" and few criminological or criminal justice trends have been so consistently documented. For the global criminological community, there is merit in conceptualizing the crime-drop as a far-reaching global experience because it focuses attention on the potential macro causes of crime and situates other global social phenomena as potential correlates. More importantly, it prompts exploration beyond specific local explanations for crime and instead (or in addition to) a consideration of the wider social and global contexts that likely underpin such a widespread experience. To be sure, most criminological theory is, itself, intended to offer a *universal* explanation for antisocial and criminal behavior. With this in mind, the crime-drop offers a rare and unique opportunity that demands scholarship with a global behavioral perspective.

It is also essential that we recognize the international experience of the crime-drop as neither a *universal* nor a *general* phenomenon. Widespread though it might be, the specific timing, location and experiences of the crime-drop are sufficiently heterogeneous to warn against its description as a truly universal or

---

[3] Includes break-and-enter dwelling, break-and-enter non-dwelling, motor vehicle theft, steal from motor vehicle, steal from retail store, steal from dwelling, steal from person, stock theft, other theft, and fraud.

[4] Includes murder, attempted murder, manslaughter, assault – domestic violence related, assault – non-domestic violence related, assault police, robbery without a weapon, robbery with a firearm, robbery with a weapon not a firearm, sexual assault and indecent assault / act of indecency / other sexual offenses.

general experience. In their study of the crime-drop, for example, van Dijk & Tseloni (2012, p. 37) caution readers from generalizing the crime-drop since in different parts of Europe the downward shift in crime manifested differently for different crime types and took effect at different times. A general cause would not likely produce such differential outcomes, they contended.

Elsewhere, scholars have also shown that different locations in close proximity, many of which share the same broad sociocultural characteristics, did not experience a drop in crime of equal measure or kind. Some experienced no drop at all. Even in Australia, not all states and territories have experienced a rapid decline in crime. In the mainland eastern states of NSW, Queensland, and Victoria, there has been a relatively consistent experience. In the Northern Territory and Western Australia, the decline has either not eventuated or been comparatively modest (ABS 2019).[5]

In our view, this heterogeneity itself serves as an important and rich source of empirical and theoretical exploration and we see value in defining the crime-drop as both a global and a local phenomenon. Without doubt, the decline in crime has been sufficiently widespread to consider the potential for some universal or general cause, yet the local experience appears meaningfully heterogeneous such that specific local contexts and potential causal mechanisms cannot be ignored. We believe that it is unlikely to be a coincidence that crime has declined in so many different parts of the world, but we also warn against overstating the potential for an all-encompassing explanation or being ignorant of the explanatory value of different local drivers.

Explaining the Crime-Drop

Not surprisingly, the macro-level data has inspired a number of significant phenomenological and theoretical contributions, each seeking to explain the crime-drop and the reasons underlying it (see for example, Farrell, 2013). Of these explanations, Kim et al. (2015) offer an organzing framework that delineates possible causes into two distinct but not mutually exclusive categories. These include *cohort effects*, or explanations that suppose an underlying change in the development of younger generations of potential offenders, and *period effects* that suppose some general exogenous environmental, cultural, or contextual factors that affect, albeit at varying degrees, all cohorts of offenders. Matthews and Minton (2018, p. 299)

---

[5] For Weisburd (2018), these seemingly micro-geographical trends complicate the crime-drop story and demand that we conceptualize crime beyond the analysis of individual-level criminal trajectories. Accordingly, a more fruitful understanding of the crime-drop may be found by treating the longitudinal experience of places, rather than individuals, as units of analysis (see also, Weisburd et al., 2004). Future research should consider this possibility, recognizing the difficulty in procuring such data over long periods of time for an entire area, state, even country.

add three additional classes of explanation, including *exogenous change* in demographics, immigration, and drug markets; *reduced opportunity* as a consequence of increased security or other target-hardening activities (see Farrell et al., 2014); and *shifting routine activities* of offenders that alter opportunity structures and patterns for offending (see also Aebi & Linde, 2010). A comprehensive study of each explanation is beyond the scope of this Element, so instead we offer a brief introduction here of potential crime-drop explanations as a prologue to our own view that developmental and life-course criminological theory offers another valuable organizing framework for theorizing the causes of the crime-drop and its potential long-term consequences.

Changing Data Recording

We begin with the simplest explanation of all – that the crime-drop is nothing more than a manifestation of changes – culturally, administratively, and ideologically – in the reporting and recording of crime and not the prevalence or incidence of actual antisocial or-rule breaking behavior. For decades, criminologists have studied the imperfect relationship between the actual occurrence of crime and its official recording (for example, Payne & Piquero, 2016; 2017). These studies most often conclude that while there is satisfactory concordance between self-reported and officially recorded crime, most criminal behavior is hidden from official view and is never recorded in the administrative apparatuses of the criminal justice system (National Academies of Sciences, 2016). The true extent of this "dark figure" (Biderman & Reiss, 1967) remains elusive and difficult to measure, but what is and is not officially recorded is not without administrative error and some systematic bias.

What contribution the underreporting and recording of crime has made to the crime-drop is unknown. Although we can only speculate, it is possible that the crime-drop reflects a wider global trend toward lower rates of reporting and recording of crime and the potential sources of this "administrative" decline in crime are many and varied. Perhaps crime victims have become complacent, apathetic, or unconvinced of the likely effectiveness of police to investigate crimes and so have simply stopped reporting them. Or, perhaps victims have found recourse and relief through online communities and social media platforms, satisfied with their digital community's validation of their victimization and thus feel less need to make official reports. Perhaps authorities have taken to responding differently to victimization reports, prioritizing only those reports with a high probability of resolution and discouraging claims that appear frivolous or difficult to investigate. It is also possible that law enforcement budgets and resources have been readjusted or reallocated in recent decades toward more intensive investigative activities (such as terrorism, white collar, and organized crime) that leave less time to pursue less serious criminal offenses and offenders.

To claim that the crime-drop is more likely a data-recording phenomenon is not to deny its empirical existence. Rather, it seeks to pay due recognition to the fact that the foundation of our empirical understanding is intimately tied to a global system of imperfect information, and that these data (and their trends) cannot be divorced from the systems from which they are created. More importantly, it recognizes that the source of the crime-drop need not be a fundamental change in criminal or antisocial behavior, but a wider shift in the manner with which both law enforcement and the community respond to crime. With few exceptions, evidence of the crime-drop has been largely evidenced through official administrative data systems and self-report offending studies are largely absent from the literature. In fact, the International Crime Victimization Survey (ICVS; van Dijk et al., 1990) provides one of the only comparative self-report studies on this topic and, while it too shows evidence of a crime-drop, its focus on crime victimization, not offending, cannot account for wider changes in community attitudes or the reporting habits of crime victims.

What is important here is to remember that the crime-drop has been almost universally explored as a reduction in criminal offending, as opposed to a reduction in the official recording of crime. It is possible that changes in both community attitudes and law enforcement practices could combine to produce a seemingly international crime-drop phenomenon with specific local variation – including the absence of such a decline in places where it might be otherwise expected. A global shift in community attitudes about victimization and victimhood, as well as changing propensities to report crime, could manifest around the globe in an increasingly online global media and social context. This, in turn, could promote a gradual reconceptualization of the self and the community. Whether this translates into less crime reporting and, therefore, less recorded crime, may depend on very specific local perceptions of trust in government institutions and the effectiveness of law enforcement. Coupled with a differential shift in policing priorities to public safety, terrorism, and international organized crime (for example, in the wake of September 11), this has the potential to provide a foreground for local variation in the manifestation of an otherwise global shift. We see less merit in the argument that some, but not all, criminal justice systems of the world have gradually shifted their data recording practices such that less actual crime is recorded in data recording systems.

Population Composition

Perhaps the most widely debated of the early crime-drop hypotheses was the proposition that crime has declined as a natural consequence of an ***aging population***. There is no other single and more stable correlate of crime than age (Hirschi & Gottfredson, 1983; Piquero et al., 2003), so it follows logically that crime should decline as the population age distribution of high-income industrialized countries edges upward. The inverted "asymmetrical bell shape" (Loeber & Farrington, 2014, p. 12) of the age-crime curve has been the object of empirical analysis since as early as Quetelet's study of French crime statistics in 1831 (2003 [1831]). The age-crime curve has since been described as "one of the brute facts of criminology" (Hirschi & Gottfredson, 1983, p. 555) and depicts the highest crime rates among those aged in their late teens and early twenties (Gottfredson & Hirschi, 1990; Loeber & Farrington, 2014). An aging population is one in which younger people comprise a diminishing proportion, either because a low birth rate has produced comparatively fewer young people (see Japan, for example) than in previous generations or because lengthening life expectancies have shifted population-level age distributions, and thus the denominator used for the calculation of crime rates.

This line of reasoning has been used in numerous studies to explain changes in violence (particularly homicide) in the United States in the 1980s and 1990s (see Fox & Piquero, 2003). During this period, homicide peaked around 1980, before declining in the early 1980s. It then rose again in the late 1980s, before falling sharply in the 1990s. Initially, a number of studies explained this trend in terms of the baby-boomer generation aging out of crime in the early 1980s, followed by their children reaching the peak age of offending in the late 1980s (Blumstein et al., 1980; Fox, 1978). However, these models proved to be less effective at explaining the decrease in violence from the early 1990s. Fox (2006) estimated that demographics explained about 10 percent of the crime-drop in the United States during the 1990s; similarly Levitt (1999) suggested that changes in the age structure accounted for no more than 1 percent per year of the fluctuations in crime rates.

Analyses elsewhere in the world have also produced mixed results. Trussler (2012) for example, found some support for a relationship between the homicide rate in Canada and the proportion of the population aged fifteen to twenty-nine years. In contrast, Hanslmaier et al. (2015) found that the population age structure in Germany explained very little of the annual variation in crime. In Australia, Weatherburn et al. (2016) argued that for the aging-population hypothesis to have sufficient merit, it would need to explain not only the crime-drop, but also the rapid increase in crime that predated it. In their conclusion, they note that the population age distribution changes were too small and too slow to have had a meaningful impact on the rise in theft and robbery prior to 2001, not to mention the rapid declines that have followed. Further, Weatherburn et al. (2016) argue that the aging Australian population should have resulted in a decline in violence at the same time as property offending, given the overrepresentation of young people in such offending, but instead violent crime remained stable for several years while property crime was well in decline.

There has also been some lengthy discussion about the **legalization of abortion** in the United States in 1973 and its specific contribution to reducing the size of the youth cohort most likely to engage in crime (Donohue & Levitt, 2001). This argument supposes that abortion services are more likely to be demanded in lower socioeconomic communities, by single and/or teen parents whose children have elsewhere been shown to be involved in crime at higher rates (Nagin et al., 1997; van Vugt et al., 2016). Following this line of inquiry, Donohue and Levitt (2001) argued that the legalization of abortion in the mid-1970s fundamentally altered the composition (not necessarily the size) of the youth population and estimated that an increase of 100 abortions per 1000 live births was associated with a 12 percent reduction in homicide, a 13 percent decline in violent crime, and a 9 percent drop in property crime. Further, the overall crime rate was estimated to be between 15 and 25 percent lower in 1997 than it would have been had abortion not been legalized.

Donohue and Levitt's analysis has not been without criticism. Fox (2006) for example, considers their study to be an insufficiently narrow use of the available data, while Blumstein (2006) noted that age cohorts change far too slowly for this factor alone to explain the sharp declines throughout 1990s. Zimring's (2007) analysis of birth rates before and after 1973 indicated that the largest change in birth rates had actually occurred well before abortion was legalized and that after 1973 birth rates actually increased steadily. These trends suggested that any drop in US crime should have happened earlier and would have likely been shorter-lived. Zimring also showed that birth rates failed to decline among single parents aged fifteen to nineteen or among African American parents – the very groups that Donohue and Levitt argued should have experienced a decline in birth rates. Of course, the legalization of abortion in the United States does not help to explain the crime-drop as an international phenomenon where in similar countries like Australia abortion remains a criminal offense in some states and territories. In NSW, for example, abortion was only repealed from the NSW Crimes Act as recently as August 2016, although since 1971 Common Law has held that medical practitioners can administer abortions under specific compassionate circumstances.[6] Weatherburn et al. (2016) argue that even if this Common Law declaration resulted in an increase in the rate of abortion in NSW, this should have affected rates of violence (as is purported in the United States), as well as rates of property crime. Instead, violent crime in NSW, specifically non-acquisitive violent offenses such as assault, remained persistently high well after the drop in property crime had started.

Another alternative explanation for the crime-drop emerged in the context of analysis in the United States that *increased immigration* has put downward pressure on crime rates because immigrants and their children have been shown to be less involved in crime. This is partly the result of migrant populations moving into less-crime-prone neighbourhoods (Sampson & Bean, 2006), but also because immigration has bolstered the number of dual-parent families in areas that have been relatively disadvantaged (Ousey & Kubrin, 2009). Several studies have shown how the decline in violent crime in the United States may have been associated with an increase in immigration. For example, Stowell et al. (2009) found that violent crime rates tended to decline in metropolitan areas where immigration became more concentrated. This finding was supported by Wadsworth (2010) who found that while increased immigration was positively associated with increases in homicide and robbery overall, cities with the largest increases in immigration between 1990 and 2000 were also the cities that experienced the largest declines. Micro-level studies also report that first-generation immigrants offend at much lower rates than second-generation and especially native-born Americans (Bersani et al., 2014).

Economic Prosperity

Growth in the US economy throughout the 1990s has received considerable attention from scholars as a possible explanation for the crime-drop. The first line of inquiry has focused on the relationship between *falling unemployment* and crime, arguing that improved personal and home finances reduce the need to pursue illicit income opportunities, that increased attachment to the institutions of employment serve to strengthen social bonds, or that being employed structurally alters routine activities and limits criminal opportunities for who are gainfully employed. Zimring (2007) for example, noted that the US unemployment rate halved between 1991 and 1999, the same time that homicide and

---

[6] The *Levine ruling*, from *R v Wald* of 1971, found abortion to be legal if a doctor had an honest and reasonable belief that, due to "any economic, social or medical ground or reason," the abortion was necessary to "preserve the woman involved from serious danger to her life or physical or mental health which the continuance of the pregnancy would entail."

robbery were in decline. Consistent with this, Raphael and Winter-Ebmer (2001) calculated that 28 percent of the decline in burglary between 1992 and 1997 could be attributed to the decline in the unemployment rate. The conclusion was also made for 82 percent of the decline in larceny, 14 percent of the decline in auto theft, and 14 percent of the decline in robbery. Contrary to Zimring's (2007) assertion, however, these authors could not conclusively link the fall in unemployment with the decline in violent crime across the United States (Raphael & Winter-Ebmer 2001). In Australia, Moffatt et al. (2005) found a significant association between the number of long-term unemployed males aged fifteen to twenty-four years and the increasing incidence of burglary and robbery in the years before the crime-drop. However, the relative improvement in unemployment after the year 2000 was likely too modest to sufficiently explain the advent of the drop and its considerable size.

In a more recent Australian analysis, Wan et al. (2012) found that unemployment was not an explanation for the decline in property and violent crime once the *improvement in average income* was taken into account. This conclusion accords with the work of Grogger (2006) who noted that the US crime-drop also coincided with an increase in the average hourly wage for sixteen to twenty-four year-old males.

Changing Drug Markets

Beyond changes in population and the economy, scholars have also sought to correlate the crime-drop with the advent of other exogenous social and environmental changes. The most prominent of these explanations relate to the changing nature of drug markets. In the United States, for example, declines in violence during the 1990s have been situated within the context of a maturing crack cocaine market and the subsequent decline in crack cocaine use. According to several drug market researchers (Johnson et al., 2005; Levitt, 2004), there was a notable relationship between the sale of crack cocaine in the late 1980s and the significant rise in gun-related violence, especially among young black men. Throughout the 1990s, the decline in homicide seemingly coincided with a decline in crack cocaine sales, leading some to conclude that the crime-drop is, perhaps, a consequence of the transformation of local drug markets (Farrell et al., 2015). A similar observation has been made in the United Kingdom where the decline in crime throughout the 1990s has been connected to a downward shift in heroin and crack cocaine use, as well as reduction in the recruitment of new users (Morgan, 2014).

The situation in Australia has been somewhat more complex, owing largely to Australia's unique experience of the heroin shortage in early 2000

(Degenhardt et al., 2006; Weatherburn et al., 2003). As has now been widely documented, Australia experienced an unprecedented fall in the availability of heroin, first on the streets of Sydney, NSW, and then later in most other capital cities. The heroin shortage coincided with the start of the crime-drop in NSW, leading Moffatt et al. (2005) to conclude that the heroin shortage (measured using non-fatal heroin overdoses as a proxy) was the single most important contributor to the crime-drop in that jurisdiction.

Changes in Policing

As the principal gatekeepers of the criminal justice system, crime rates are not surprisingly sensitive to global, national, and local policing priorities. There is no universal approach to the allocation and utilization of policing resources, and current policing practices can vary significantly even between bordering counties and policing commands. Over time, policing priorities have shifted, as have their implementation strategies, and these changes offer possible insight into why crime has declined.

Certainly in the United States, researchers have sought to identify what role the increase in police numbers has played in driving crime rates down. Zimring (2012), for example, argued that changes to the size and activities of the police in New York was one of the principal reasons for why the crime-drop in that state was larger than almost any other comparable city. Specifically, Zimring (2012) reports a 44 percent increase in New York Police Department staffing between 1990 and 1999 (with a particularly large increase in those working on narcotics-related issues), a shift to tactics that focused on quality-of-life issues (but which were expected to net serious offenders), and improved resource accountability with the introduction of Compstat (a process for matching police activity with crime patterns – especially serious crime – most commonly referred to as hot-spots policing).[7]

Analysis by Roeder et al. (2015) suggested that while the increase in police numbers across the United States is likely to have contributed up to 10 percent of the crime-drop, the use of Compstat-style approaches had produced crime-prevention dividends that were larger in some places than others. In the cities where Compstat was employed, Roeder et al. estimated that the use of Compstat was associated with a 13 percent decline in violent crime, 11 percent decline in property crime, and a 13 percent decline in homicide.

---

[7] Other research in policing shows that it matters less how many officers there are, but instead what the officers do on the street that relates to crime reductions (see, e.g., Kovandzic et al., 2016; Sherman, 1995).

It should be noted here that the evidence supporting the differential benefit of Compstat is far from settled and more recent work has cast some doubt as to the veracity of some of the earlier claims about its resounding effectiveness (see Weisburd et al., 2019, for a review). Braga and Weisburd (2019) argue that much of the impact previously attributed to Compstat was framed through its capacity to support problem-oriented policing and other proactive policing strategies. However, Weisburd et al. (2019) point out that the emphasis on control and command in the innovation led to restrictions on the development of innovative problem solving approaches. Contrary to Roeder et al. (2015), the inconclusive evidence of effectiveness significantly weakens the proposition that Compstat-style innovations were solely responsible for the decline in crime ·across the United States.

In Australia, Weatherburn et al. (2016) showed that police numbers in NSW rose by about 20 percent between 2001 and 2003, but have remained relatively stable for the decade thereafter. The increase in the number of officers earlier in the period of decline might not, alone, be expected to drive crime rates down significantly. To the contrary, increasing police numbers have the potential to increase crime rates as the detention rates for on-the-street, status, and disorderly conduct offenses increase with the greater police presence. That said, if coupled with improvements to the quality of the policing activity, this has the potential to increase arrest rates for serious offenses, leading to a heightened perception of detection among potential offenders and, consequently, an increase in both general and specific deterrence. Wan et al. (2012), for example, demonstrated how the increased arrest and clearance rate in NSW had reduced both violent and property crime, presumably as a consequence of both incapacitation and deterrence effects. According to the authors, a 10 percent increase in the arrest rate was associated with 1.4 percent reduction in property crime and a 3.0 percent reduction in violent crime across NSW.

Such has been the recent interest in policing practice and crime prevention that in 2015 the National Academy of Sciences convened the *Committee on Proactive Policing: Effects on Crime, Communities, and Civil Liberties.* The committee was tasked with the responsibility of reviewing the evidence on the success on different proactive policing strategies – most of which had been published in the wider context of the US crime-drop over the last three decades. In the Committee's final report (National Academies of Sciences, Engineering, and Medicine 2018), four main types of proactive policing strategies were assessed, each with mixed or favorable outcomes. While it is beyond the scope of this Element to summarize these findings in full, we note the Committee's consistent finding about the positive short-term effectiveness of proactive policing strategies and the mixed or limited evidence of long-term impacts. We suggest that the

Committee's report, coupled with the evidence from Australia, is a good reminder that increasing police numbers is unlikely to have contributed to the sustained drop in crime if such an increase was not met with a wider commitment to innovation in policing practice, or what the police do (see Sherman, 1995). To the extent that proactive policing has contributed to the crime decline across the globe, it is likely not the only explanation for the longer-term trend.

Increased Imprisonment

The role of imprisonment in explaining the crime-drop has been extensively examined in the United States, where declines in both property and violent crime coincided with significant increases in the use of imprisonment as a criminal justice sanction (Donohue, 2009; Marvell & Moody, 1994; Spelman, 1994). Spelman's (2000) analysis of four studies that were considered methodologically robust found that a 10 percent increase in the prison population would likely reduce aggregate crime rates by between 1.6 and 3.1 percent. Further work by Levitt (2004) that examined the impact of imprisonment between 1991 and 2001, concluded that increases in the prison population accounted for a 12 percent reduction in homicide and violent crime and an 8 percent reduction in property crime.

Drawing on more recent evidence, Roeder et al. (2015) noted the importance of accounting for the diminishing marginal returns associated with imprisonment, with the impact of incarceration falling as the prison population rises. Their analysis indicated that increased incarceration had no impact on violent crime between 1990 and 2013. Where property crime was concerned, it accounted for approximately 6 percent of the decline between 1990 and 1999 and just 0.2 percent of the decline between 2000 and 2013. Similar diminishing marginal returns were observed in the United States by Liedka et al. (2006). In Australia, Moffatt et al. (2005) found a significant relationship between increasing total time of imprisonment for burglary and the number of burglary offenses. However, a more sophisticated model using NSW data found no relationship between prison sentence length and rates of property and violent crime (Wan et al., 2012). Instead, this study showed that the *rate* of imprisonment was associated with rates of crime. A 1 percent increase in the rate of imprisonment was estimated to result in a 0.12 percent reduction in property crime and a 0.17 percent reduction in violent crime.

Overall, the link between incarceration and the crime-drop is confused and requires further empirical qualification. In the main, this confusion stems from a lack of clarity about the underlying causal mechanism of imprisonment in a context of diminishing crime rates. For example, the role of imprisonment may be to remove or incapacitate high volume offenders from the active offender population. Or imprisonment might reduce the longer-term reoffending rates of the highest volume offenders. Or the threat of imprisonment might deter other less-serious offenders from escalating to higher volumes of crime. In the United States, the crime-reducing capacity of increased sentence lengths has been questioned (Durlauf & Nagin, 2011; Piquero & Blumstein, 2007; Durlauf & Nagin, 2010), and there is little evidence that imprisonment reduces the recidivism of high-volume offenders (Cullen et al., 2011). To the contrary, it seems imprisonment likely results in an increase in offending. As for the deterrent effect of imprisonment, the evidence is mixed, although the perceived certainty of punishment is considered the most likely link between higher incarceration rates and lower rates of crime (Durlauf & Nagin, 2011).

Increased Securitization

Over the past thirty years, there has been a significant increase in the prevalence and effectiveness of security, which may have simply increased the effort involved in committing property crime and thereby contributed to the decline in that offense type. Improved security has been particularly highlighted in relation to the reduction in vehicle theft (Brown, 2015b; Farrell et al., 2011; Farrell & Brown, 2016) and burglary (van Dijk & Vollaard, 2012; Tseloni et al., 2014).

Farrell et al. (2011) have put forward two hypotheses for how securitization may have reduced crime more generally (and not just property crime). The "debut crime" hypothesis suggests that improved security particularly influenced the kinds of crimes that young people engage in at the start of a criminal career (such as vehicle theft). By making these types of offenses more difficult to commit, improved security has prevented young people from engaging in crime and subsequently going on to commit more serious crime. Drawing on US data, Farrell et al. (2015) have shown that, across a variety of offense types, the decline in crime between 1980 and 2010 was greatest among young people.

The second hypothesis, the "keystone crime" hypothesis, argues that more serious crime is prevented by focusing on those that are less serious. For example, bank robberies may be prevented because vehicles (for use in the getaway) cannot be stolen, and drug offenses may be prevented because offenders are unable to commit property crime (such as burglary) to obtain the cash needed to buy drugs. Although intriguing, this hypothesis remains largely untested.

In Australia, improved security was the most frequent reason given by police detainees to explain the property crime-drop (Brown, 2015a). Other studies have also drawn a connection between improved vehicle security and reductions in vehicle theft in Australia (Farrell et al., 2011; Kriven & Ziersch, 2007; MM Starrs, 2002; National Motor Vehicle Theft Reduction Council, 2007; Potter & Thomas, 2001).

Decline in Risky Behavior

Another compelling argument comes from those scholars looking at broader trends in risky behavior, many of which also appear to be declining in prevalence and incidence among younger generations and cohorts. Mishra and Lalumière (2009), for example, have suggested that the reduction in crime is actually part of a wider trend that has seen reductions in a range of risky behaviors, not just those that are criminally sanctioned. Reductions in violent crime in the United States and Canada were found to be associated with reductions in motor vehicle accidents, risky sexual behavior, and rates of school drop-out. In Australia, Livingston et al. (2016) conducted a comprehensive age-period cohort analysis of alcohol use using the National Drug Strategy Household Survey. In their analysis they found strong evidence of a decline in alcohol participation among cohorts born after 1990, as well as a substantial decline in the average volume of alcohol consumed by younger drinkers. This Australian data on alcohol consumption is consistent with trends in Europe (Norström, & Svensson, 2014; Radaev & Roshchina 2019; Raninen et al., 2014; Törrönen et al., 2019)[8] and correlates with similar reductions in the prevalence of other drug use (Han et al., 2017). This suggests that explanations for the crime-drop must also take account of these seemingly simultaneous changes in other forms of risky behavior. As Duell et al. (2018) note, despite some geographical heterogeneity in the age-graded manifestation of specific types of risky behavior, there is a strong general and geographically homogenous risk-propensity curve that functions much like the age-crime curve (see Duell et al., 2018; Farrington & Loeber, 2014).

Environmental Explanations

Environmental factors are defined here as those that relate to changes in the wider environment in which individuals reside that may influence their propensity for involvement in crime. Perhaps the most widely debated of these explanations concerns the prevalence and intensity of childhood exposure to lead. Exposure to high concentrations of lead, for example, has been linked to

---

[8] The evidence from North America is mixed in this regard and depends on sampling (see Grucza et al., 2018).

a wide range of adverse physiological and psychosocial outcomes, including deficits in central nervous system functioning (Needleman et al., 1990) and region-specific loss of cerebral volume (Cecil et al., 2011) leading to a range of visual, visuospatial, verbal, memory, attention, and motor-functioning deficits (Vlasak et al., 2019; Sanders et al., 2009). These physiological changes have subsequently been correlated with poorer psychosocial and cognitive outcomes, including higher rates of impulsivity, anxiety, and depression (Winter & Sampson 2017), as well as poorer education outcomes (Chandramouli et al., 2009), higher rates of interpersonal aggression (Dietrich et al., 2001), and increased contact with the criminal justice system (Wright et al., 2008).

With strong evidence linking childhood lead exposure to antisocial behavior and aggression in adolescence and adulthood, it follows that the removal of lead from petrol (and later from household paints) in the United States in the 1970s was to have a positive impact on crime rates throughout the 1990s. Reyes (2007), for example, estimated that by limiting childhood lead exposure, there was a 56 percent decline in violent crime across the United States. Farrell et al. (2010) however, have noted that while this temporal correlation fits with the US experience, it does not marry so well with the crime-drop experience of other countries in Europe and the Pacific. In Australia, Weatherburn et al. (2016) argue that the timing of reduction in lead fits poorly with the observed reductions in property crime and even more poorly with the observed reductions in violent crime.

With these potential explanations in hand, we next turn to what we believe is a complementary but especially unique potential explanation for understanding the crime-drop. Specifically, we advance the possibility that the crime-drop can be partially explained through a developmental/life-course lens.

2 The "Crime-Drop" through a Developmental Lens

Many of the attempts to explain the crime-drop have thus far focused on those factors that are thought to have resulted in a decline in the offending frequency of existing adult offenders. In doing so, this line of research has been focused on understanding why already active offenders might have transitioned to committing less crime or why previously high-volume offenders may have desisted early from their criminal careers. In Australia, for example, the heroin shortage, coupled with increasing rates of employment and an ever-constricting stolen-goods market (Weatherburn et al., 2016) are each thought to have acted as cocontributors to the local crime-drop – driving a formerly high-volume, drug-using offender population into treatment and out of the criminal justice system as the need for illicit income decreased and the risk of transacting in stolen goods increased. What is missing from these contemporary explanations, however, is some account of the growing empirical evidence that the crime-drop is more likely the result of fewer young offenders embarking on criminal careers than it is older offenders desisting. In this section, we consider the merits of developmental and life-course theories of crime and their potential value in helping to understand both the causes and consequences of the crime-drop phenomenon. To our knowledge, only two studies to date have taken a life-course approach. Both suggest that the crime-drop may be explained by a reduction in adolescent-limited offending (Weatherburn et al., 2014; Farrell et al., 2015), however, in both cases, the authors used aggregate cross-sectional data, which has meant that it was not possible to determine whether the observed reductions in adolescent offending were due to changes in frequency, prevalence, or a combination of both.

The Crime-Drop as a "Youth" Phenomenon

To appreciate the potential value of a developmental and life-course approach to understanding the crime-drop, it is important to recall that for all empirical data now available, one feature of the international crime-drop experience has emerged as surprisingly consistent. The crime-drop, it seems, has been significantly driven by a rapid decline in rates of crime among youth populations. Blumstein (2006), for example, showed that declining youth arrest rates were a significant contributor to the recorded fall in homicide across the United States, while the same has been shown for other violent crimes (Cook & Laub 2002) and total arrest rates (Kim et al., 2015). Similarly, Farrell et al. (2015) explored the age-specific profiles of crime across multiple offense types and also concluded that within the aggregate crime-drop there was a disproportionate drop in crime among the youngest age groups. In Europe, youth arrest rates have also been shown to be a significant driver of the aggregate crime-drop, including in England and Wales (Soothill et al., 2008; Morgan, 2014), Denmark (Andersen et al., 2016), Sweden (von Hofer, 2014), and Scotland (Matthews and Minton 2018). In Australia, researchers have also remarked at the disproportionate decline in youth crime rates (Weatherburn et al., 2014) and the need to understand the crime-drop through the lens of youth development (Payne et al., 2018).

This seemingly consistent conclusion about the disproportionate decline in youth crime rates has been strengthened in the context of less convincing and less consistent evidence about the fall in rates of crime in adult populations. Farrell et al. (2015) for example, showed that for offenders in their thirties, violent and property crime rates in the United States actually increased during the early phases of the crime-drop. Using total arrest rates, Kim et al. (2015) also demonstrated the same for those in their forties, despite Blumstein's (2006) conclusion that US homicide rates had declined across all age categories. In an analysis of data from England and Wales (Morgan 2014) and Scotland (Matthew & Minton 2018), studies have shown that during the UK crime-drop, conviction and cautioning rates increased among those aged over thirty, while in Denmark, Andersen et al. (2016) showed that conviction rates declined among older offenders, but at a much less substantial rate than was seen in the younger-age cohorts.

Period and Cohort – Continuity and Change

In recognizing the crime-drop as a predominantly youth-based phenomenon, one that has strengthened with the emergence of new youth cohorts, our search for explanations must be revisited and potentially reconsidered. As noted, much of the explanatory work so far has been in the pursuit of "period" effects, which situate the sudden and rapid decline of crime as a result of some combination of exogenous factors that have exerted downward pressure on the frequency of criminal offending (improving economy, changing drug markets, increased use of incarceration, more police, etc.). Period effects are appealing because they are often identified as relatively rapid events that, if temporally aligned, seem to offer a more fitting account of the crime-drop phenomenon. "Cohort" effects, on the other hand, are those that seek to explain the crime-drop through observed empirical changes in developing cohorts of the population, the assumption being that newer cohorts of the population are less inclined to crime or have lower levels of criminal propensity. They are, at present, the least favored of the two categories, mostly because the dominant causal cohort mechanisms (i.e., the legalization of abortion and the reduction in the use of lead) have relatively little empirical support and because the degree of change required to produce the crime-drop was too large, and needed to have occurred too rapidly, to be explained by the normally small and incremental changes that are seen in emerging cohorts of the population.

The developing picture of an increasingly youth-based crime-drop, however, demands a fresh look at the potential merits of cohort-based explanations and the need to integrate period and cohort effects into a more comprehensive explanatory framework. Notably, this debate about the relative merits of "period" and "cohort" effects on the international crime-drop has an interesting parallel within the criminal career debates of the 1980s (see review in Piquero et al., 2003). Sparked by a disagreement about the relationship between age and crime, as well as the necessity for longitudinal data, the criminal career framework outlined by Blumstein et al. (1986) became a vehicle for a much larger discussion concerning the fundamental nature of individual-level, as opposed to aggregate-level offending over the life course. This discussion centered on two seemingly incongruent and contradictory empirical findings regarding the coexistence of both "continuity" and "change" in criminal offending. Continuity, elsewhere described as persistent between-individual differences or persistent population heterogeneity, has long been a staple of criminological theorizing and subsequent empirical research. Dominated by cross-sectional research studies, early criminologists offered mostly structural and static theories to elucidate the apparent disparities between offenders and nonoffenders as identified in their research studies. These included the various incarnations of strain theory (Agnew, 1992, 1997; Cloward & Ohlin, 1960; Merton, 1938; Rosenfeld & Messner, 1995), social disorganization theory (Bursik, 1988; Markowitz et al., 2001; Sampson & Groves, 1989), differential association theory (Burgess & Akers, 1966; Matsueda, 1988, 2001), and social control or social bond theory (Hirschi, 1986, 1998). Since the primary aim of this cross-sectional research was to identify differences between individuals at a single time point, it is not surprising that these subsequent explanations sought to connect the apparent between-individual differences in criminal participation to the various social structures and influences that were identified as having defined their life experiences. Continuity, in the criminological sense, describes those differences between individuals that seem to persist throughout life; differences that manifest in relatively more or less involvement in crime at all ages.

Paradoxically, longitudinal data and their associated research methodologies have also emphasized the importance and ubiquity of change and its coexistence with continuity has since been the lifeblood of developmental debates in criminology. Robins (1978, p. 611) for example, articulated this problem clearly when she observed that "adult antisocial behavior virtually requires childhood antisocial behavior [continuity], yet most antisocial children do not become antisocial adults [change]." Later described by Cohen and Vila (1996) as the "paradox of persistence" (see also Ezell & Cohen, 2005), what Robins (1978) describes is the difficult challenge faced by criminologists in the wake of mounting empirical evidence that crime is a consequence of both continuity in between-individual differences and change within individuals over time (Caspi & Moffitt, 1995; Cernkovich & Giordano, 2001; Cline, 1980; Gove, 1985; Loeber & Le Blanc, 1990; McCord, 1980; Robins & Rutter, 1990; Rutter, Quinton, & Hill, 1990; Sampson, 2000; Tracy & Kempf-Leonard, 1996). In the developmental criminological tradition, change is the consequence of two possible mechanisms: the diminishing opportunities for crime that occur with age (Gottfredson & Hirschi, 1990) or the state dependence processes that causally link temporal or exogenous events to a shift in individual propensities for crime.

Theoretical efforts to explain continuity and change have elsewhere been summarized into a conceptual framework that delineates persistent population heterogeneity and state-dependence into a tripartite classification (see Paternoster et al., 1997). These include general-static theories, general-dynamic theories, and developmental/taxonomic theories, each of which is then differentiated with reference to two key principles. The first is whether a theory posits a single or multiple causal mechanism(s) and the second is whether the hypothesised cause(s) of crime can change over the age distribution. Accordingly, theories positing a single underlying cause of crime are considered "general," while those with multiple causes are considered typological or taxonomic. Where the hypothesized cause of crime is fixed at all ages, the theory is considered "static," whereas a "dynamic" theory is one in which the nature or strength of the causal mechanism varies with age. General-static theories argue that crime is caused by a single (general) causal mechanism and is the same for all offenders and at all ages. The most famous general-static account of crime was developed by Gottfredson and Hirschi (1990) in their widely cited *General Theory of Crime*. Here, they describe population heterogeneity as the persistent between-individual differences in criminal propensity that result from poor parenting and ineffective childrearing practices during the formative developmental years. They contend that their theory is general because it offers one explanatory construct – self-control – which is "meant to explain all crimes, at all times, and for that matter, many other forms of behavior that are not sanctioned by the state" (Gottfredson & Hirschi, 1990, p. 117). In essence, Gottfredson and Hirschi offer their own form of control theory to explain the longitudinal course of criminal involvement and, like all control theories, their theory implies that individuals are typically restrained from engaging in antisocial activities by some prevailing and controlling force that, when absent, frees individuals to engage in activities that defy prosocial norms. Those who do so on a frequent basis are described by Gottfredson and Hirschi (1990, pp. 90–91) as inclined to commit antisocial acts in the pursuit of self-interest because they lack the ability to resist temptation, they persistently seek immediate and easy gratification, and they are "impulsive, insensitive, physical (as opposed to mental), risk taking, short sighted, and nonverbal." For these individuals, low self-control results from less than favorable child-rearing and parenting environments that lack adequate supervision, have minimal behavior monitoring, and have insufficient or inconsistent disciplinary practices (Gottfredson & Hirschi, 1990, p. 97). Children who grow up in such environments are said to be the products of failed socialization; having not learned the skills necessary to ensure that they are able to delay gratification, to empathize with others, and to sacrifice their own personal needs for the well-being of those around them.

To explain the coexistence of continuity and change over the life-course, the General Theory is set within a propensity–event framework (Gottfredson, 2005). It delineates self-control (propensity) from the opportunity structures (events) that precipitate crime. Continuity exists because underlying propensity to engage in antisocial behavior differentiates individuals along a continuum that is not malleable over time. In other words, according to Gottfredson and Hirschi's perspective an individual's self-control is highly unlikely to change regardless of their age.[9] Where change in actual offending is evidenced, it is not because of some fundamental shift in a person's propensity to engage in crime, but rather, from the changing socialization and environmental cues that influence the opportunity structures (situational and environmental) that typically give rise to crime. In this case, age is seen as having a global effect on the opportunity structures that facilitate crime because "the rate at which socialization continues to occur is approximately the same for everyone" (Nagin & Paternoster, 2000, p. 122). Moreover, the seemingly high correlation between unfavorable adolescent and adulthood situations (including alcohol and drug use) results not from any special causal process, but because individuals with low levels of self-control will essentially self-select into situations and scenarios consistent with this latent characteristic (Ezell & Cohen, 2005; Nagin & Paternoster, 2000).

General-dynamic theories similarly argue that the cause of crime is singular and general to all offenders, but that the cause can vary in strength and kind, consequent to exogenous influences and state-dependent effects. Sampson and Laub's (1993) Age-graded Informal Social Control Theory is the most prominent of these general-dynamic approaches in which the authors offer informal social control as the single cause of crime, but insist that change in adulthood occurs as the relative strength and sources of that social control vary with age. To be sure, Sampson and Laub's work was focused primarily on adulthood transitions and in doing so sought to identify the life factors and processes (such as marriage, employment, and military service) that encouraged criminal persistence and delayed criminal desistence. As a result, they pay only limited attention to early childhood and adolescent development, except insofar as early childhood experiences are said to provide the foundation for explaining the

---

[9] Contrary to these theorists, there is evidence that self-control is more malleable than fixed and is responsive to interventions (see Piquero et al., 2010).

relative stability (or continuity) in between-individual offending during adulthood. In their view, the development of adolescent antisocial behavior results from a weakening of the informal social controls connected to family, peers, and the school environment. In the family, for example, low levels of parental supervision; erratic, threatening, and harsh discipline practices; and weak parental attachment predict adolescent antisocial behavior (Sampson & Laub, 1997). Structural and early childhood factors, such as family poverty, neuropsychological deficits, hyperactivity, and low self-control play an important, but indirect role as they serve to weaken the attachment of a child to their social environment. This weakening of social bonds occurs through a process described as "interactional continuity," where the cycle of negative reinforcement perpetuates the accumulation of disadvantage, which in turn erodes one's ability to develop and strengthen attachment to prosocial institutions and enhances opportunities for continued antisocial behavior. In adulthood, change is ubiquitous and results from changes in informal social controls.

Having attributed between-individual stability in offending to weak social attachment, Sampson and Laub then explain how the social ties embedded into adult life transitions have relative influence on the decisions made by offenders to engage in antisocial and criminal activities. Accordingly, they argue that if such transitions strengthen an individual's ties to conventional social institutions, then they have the potential to interrupt the cycle of accumulated disadvantage. If they weaken an individual's attachment to prosocial bonds, they are likely to influence the commission of further offending. This, Sampson and Laub (1997) suggest, is reason to believe that while "individual traits and childhood experiences are important for understanding behavioral stability, experiences in adolescence and adulthood can redirect criminal trajectories in either a more positive or negative manner" (1997, p. 170).

Another approach defined within the general-dynamic framework is Farrington's (2005a) Integrated Cognitive and Antisocial Potential (ICAP) model, in which it is theorized that all individuals possess a degree of underlying antisocial potential, the translation of which into actual antisocial behavior depends on cognitive processes that are affected by a range of social, environmental, and situational cues. The theory's key construct is described by Farrington (2005b) as "antisocial potential" (AP) that exists in two forms – long-term AP and short-term AP. In much the same way that the General Theory posits self-control as a general cause of between-individual variability (Gottfredson & Hirschi, 1990), Farrington explains that long-term AP develops during early childhood and remains as an undercurrent of causality to explain between-individual differences across the life-course. It may result from a combination of biological, genetic, and structural influences like strain, socialization, neuropsychological deficits, and behavioral traits.

Not dissimilar to self-control in the General Theory, Farrington (2005b) argues that all individuals maintain a degree of long-term AP such that they can be ordered on a continuum from high to low. At all ages, an individual with high levels of long-term AP will be relatively more likely to engage in antisocial behavior than those with low levels. The absolute value of AP peaks during adolescence because of the changing nature of those factors that influence the development of long-term AP. Peer networks, for example, become increasingly more important, while parental bonds become less so.

For Farrington (2005b), the question of "how offenders develop" is quite separate from the question of "why offenders commit crime," and although both are in many ways interconnected, it is argued that long-term AP cannot be the only explanatory factor. Instead, the ICAP model suggests that in addition to accumulated long-term AP, individuals also experience varying degrees of short-term AP that are influenced by the structure of antisocial and criminal opportunities, the presence of suitable victims, and a range of "energizing factors," such as being bored, drunk, or "egged-on" by peers (Farrington, 2005b). The translation of both short and long-term AP into criminal activities depends on cognitive decision-making processes whereby the subjective costs and benefits of the antisocial act are weighed against each other, taking account of the immediate situational (likely material gain and probability of being detected) and social (disapproval by parents and partners, or approval by peers) factors. Feedback loops exist such that the consequences of engaging in antisocial activities may further contribute to the development of higher or lower levels of long-term AP and consequently affect the criminal decision-making process depending on their reinforcing or punishing qualities. If, for example, the formal sanctions received as a result of detection by the police result in further labelling and stigmatization, this may limit future opportunities for gainful employment and increase the divide between economic means and goals. By extension, this increases strain and contributes to long-term AP.

The final classification of developmental and life-course theories are those taxonomic or "trajectory" based theories that treat population heterogeneity and state-dependence as multi-causal constructs that vary between different groups of offenders. Perhaps the most influential typological account of crime was developed by Terrie Moffitt in her dual taxonomy of antisocial behavior (Moffitt, 1993, 1994, 1997). Using data from a representative cohort of 1,037 children born in New Zealand between 1972 and 1973, Moffitt (1993) offers an explanatory model of the age-crime curve built around two distinct offender groupings, each possessing a unique natural history of antisocial behavior over the life-course. The first group was described as "life-course persistent"; offenders whose criminality is frequent, long-term, and occasionally serious. Commencing antisocial behavior at a young age, this small group (of less than 8 to 10 percent of the total offending population) engages in antisocial behavior "of one sort or another at every stage of life" and for this reason they "make up the childhood and adulthood tails of the age-crime curve" (Moffitt, 1997, p. 13).

The factors influencing the development of life-course persistent offending are found in early childhood, where according to Moffitt (1997), there is the "juxtaposition of a vulnerable and difficult infant with an adverse rearing context" such that "the challenge of coping with a difficult child evokes a chain of failed parent/child encounters" (p. 17). This so-called transactional process promotes the development of an underlying antisocial personality that, according to Moffitt (1993, 1997), can often be traced back to early childhood risk factors such as neuropsychological deficits, difficult or hyperactive temperament, high levels of impulsivity, low verbal IQ, and poor self-control.

For these life-course persistent offenders, the persistence of antisocial behavior throughout adolescence and into adulthood occurs for two reasons. First, the early neuropsychological factors underpinning the development of an antisocial personality are difficult to extinguish. For example, hyperactivity and low self-control in the teenage years may manifest in acts of truancy and school-yard bullying, while in adulthood they may manifest in workplace absenteeism and domestic and family violence, just to name a few. Second, antisocial behavior has "cumulative consequences" for the future. Those who continue to engage in antisocial activities fail to learn prosocial alternatives, fail to affiliate with prosocial peers and institutions, or otherwise accumulate antisocial labels that "foreclose later opportunities" for positive social interaction (Moffitt, 1997, p. 23). As the years progress, they continue to accumulate disadvantage and thus become entwined in a lifestyle that further promotes their continued antisocial involvement.

The second classification in Moffitt's dual taxonomy describes a much larger group of offenders whose antisocial expressions occur mainly during adolescence and are sporadic and inconsistent across situations. These offenders are called "adolescent-limited" offenders since the hallmark of their criminal activity is its restriction to adolescence and its notable discontinuity in adulthood; they are the reason the age-crime curve peaks during the adolescent years. In many respects, these adolescent-limited offenders are almost indistinguishable from their life-course persistent peers during adolescence with respect to their antisocial involvement. They tend to commit just as many crime types at roughly equal frequency, however, they will generally fail to exhibit any of the significant neuropsychological deficits or behavioral problems that underpin life-course persistent offending and refrain from serious, person-oriented offenses. By their mid-twenties, they will have ceased criminal activity altogether (Moffitt, 1993).

The willingness of the adolescent-limited group to engage in antisocial behavior is largely encouraged through antisocial peer socialization. Their crime is typically characterized as an act of social mimicry; imitating the behaviors and activities of other antisocial peers in an effort to bridge the "maturity gap" between one's social and biological age (Moffitt & Caspi, 2001). This desire to achieve early maturational status, and the subsequent power and privilege it bestows, acts to positively encourage and reinforce antisocial and criminal behavior because such activities symbolize independence and maturity among youth (Moffitt, 1997). As they move beyond adolescence and into adulthood however, these adolescent-limited offenders experience a gradual loss of motivation for delinquency as they exit the maturity gap and begin to attain traditional adult statuses and roles such as marriage and employment. The adult privileges that they coveted with such earnestness during their youth are now easily accessible to them and so the consequences of their criminal activity shift from being positively rewarding to potentially punishing (Moffitt, 1997). Underpinning this motivational change are contingency and commitment costs – defined by Moffitt (1993, 1997) as the personal assessment of the risk of formal and informal sanctions compared to the likely benefits of the criminal action in question. These adolescent-limited offenders can cease their offending with relative ease because, unlike their life-course persistent peers, they have no underlying neuropsychological deficit or accumulated antisocial personality to limit the development of prosocial bonds or to hinder their attachment to prosocial institutions.

The distinguishing feature of Moffitt's dual taxonomic approach is the discrete classification of two population offender profiles. Although her theory draws upon many other explanatory models (differential association, labelling, and social control), it uses these ideas to predict two somewhat divergent life-course offending trajectories: one short-lived, affected primarily by socialization factors, and constrained to the adolescent years; the other starting in early childhood, caused by underlying behavioral traits, and persisting over the life-course. Both trajectories are qualitatively different from each other, not just in form, but also in etiology. Life-course persistent offending, for example, finds its roots in the stability and longevity of neuropsychological deficit and disadvantaged developmental environments, while adolescent-limited offending results from the changing nature of socialization and strain factors that are exacerbated at times when adolescents experience a differential between their desired social and biological age (Moffitt, 1997).

Aims of This Study

Developmental and life-course theory, and its unique theoretical intersection of both period and cohort effects, offers a new lens through which the international crime-drop phenomenon can be analyzed, especially in Australia, the context of our research. Drawing on the criminal career and offender trajectory approaches, this study seeks to describe how the prevalence, frequency, onset, and types of offenses have changed between two Australian birth cohorts. These cohorts, born in 1984 and 1994, have been selected because their adolescence was contextually different, straddling the now widely documented crime-drop in NSW (2001). By delving into the longitudinal offending patterns of these two birth cohorts and examining how their composition and trajectories have changed in just ten years, this study offers a unique opportunity to revisit existing explanations and potentially build new ones from a developmental and life-course (DLC) perspective.

First, all DLC approaches recognize the importance of between-individual behavioral stability and most tie these persistent differences to some underlying distribution of criminal or antisocial propensity. The seemingly universal nature of the international crime-drop raises questions about the nature of this latent distribution, whether it has changed in functional form, or whether it has weakened across the population as a result of improved parenting, enhanced opportunities for pro-socialization, or more effective early interventions. Whether there has been some population-wide shift in antisocial propensity might be revealed if the differences between our two birth cohorts are universal to all offenders and general to all sub-groups of the birth population.

Second, DLC theories place significant emphasis on the value of opportunity structures and the temporal or situational factors that energize offending, but largely agree that the relative importance (to the individual) of these state-dependent effects will vary depending on the level and degree of preexisting antisocial propensity. Support for this proposition may be found if the differences between our cohorts exist only (or at least principally) within specific offense types and within specific offender groups. If chronic offenders – those who are likely motivated by strong antisocial propensities – do not change in prevalence, frequency, onset, or offense mix throughout the crime-drop, but their low or moderate offending peers do change, then this will offer support to the view that crime dropped because criminal activity became less rewarding, less fun, and less likely to meet the immediate needs of the normative adolescent in development. Further, it might also point to the emergence of new opportunity structures that have provided alternative outlets for antisocial activity (i.e., via internet bullying, access to online pornography, etc.) that is not policed or subject to formal surveillance and detection.

Third, DLC researchers have long identified the timing of criminal onset and the mix of offending types as providing strong signals for the likely unfolding of future criminal trajectories. To what extent the onset of offending has changed between our cohorts, both in timing and offense type, and whether these changes relate to consistent longitudinal predictions, will shed important light on potential causes of the crime-drop as well also its longer-term consequences. For example, if the prevalence of violent-offending onset and property-offending onset change at different rates (between the cohorts), or if violent-offending onset does not change at all, then there is a potentially strong argument for securitization as a principal cause of the crime-drop. If, however, the prevalence of non-property offending onset also declines, then this would add weight to those more general, developmental, and cohort-wide causes. In a sense, this approach attempts to explicate crime signatures that may support particular theoretical positions (Eck & Madensen, 2009)

Fourth, DLC researchers have long pointed to the need for early interventions and diversion programs to limit the accumulation of disadvantage (Sampson & Laub 1993), to prevent ensnaring (Moffitt 1997), or to limit the development of long-term antisocial potential (Farrington 2003). This investment might have contributed to the crime-drop if the criminogenic nature of criminal justice contact has been muted through policy efforts that have lower crime frequencies, and encouraged earlier desistance (see Olds et al., 1998). The potential contribution of these efforts will be signaled in this study if the probabilities of escalation and persistence have changed between cohorts, especially among the earliest onset offenders.

Finally, as noted earlier, we offer one of only a small number of comparative birth cohort studies in criminology. The most recent study prior to ours was the research conducted in the United States by Fabio and colleagues (2006) who explored two cohorts from the Pittsburgh Youth Study. In their work, the authors exploit the generational differences in violence and their analysis provides a useful comparison to our own.

3 Data and Methodology

Research Design

The objective of this research is to examine whether, in the context of the crime-drop, there has been a significant change in the prevalence, frequency, and nature of police contact among young people in NSW, Australia. We use a longitudinal approach to examine the experience of two NSW-born birth cohorts (separated in birth by ten years) and their experiences of police contact during adolescence and early adulthood. Our longitudinal approach is unique in studies of the crime decline and the analysis herein adds value to the existing research on this topic; research that has almost exclusively relied on the examination of temporal changes using aggregate crime rates or repeated cross-sectional data.

Data

The data for this study were extracted from the NSW Bureau of Crime Statistics and Research (BOCSAR) Reoffending Database (ROD) using the names and dates of birth of all those born in NSW in 1984 and 1994. To facilitate the data extraction, a full register of live births was obtained from the NSW Registry of Births Deaths and Marriages, an approach that is consistent with previous studies of the 1984 birth cohort (Hua et al., 2006). For each individual on the two registers, a data match was performed to extract the offense-level unit records, together with offense-specific details such as the offense type, date, and outcome. A series of demographic variables was also extracted from both the births register and the ROD database. This includes the individual's biological sex recorded at birth and Indigenous status.

Counting Rules

For the purpose of the present study, criminal offending is counted for each unique offense that was "proven." Proven offenses are those recorded by the police as having an official outcome that substantiated the offense. In most cases, this constitutes the recording of a formal conviction by a court, however it may also include formal cautions or diversions where the offense is not disputed. All unique offense counts are included in this study, meaning that where an offender is apprehended and charged with multiple counts of the same offense, these are recorded as separate offenses. Finally, crime types are coded using the Australian and New Zealand Standard Offense Classification (ANZSOC 2014).

Age-specific and cumulative prevalence rates are calculated relative to the population count in each birth cohort. As extracted from the NSW Registry of Births Deaths and Marriages, these were 83,328 in 1984 and 89,373 in 1994. At the time of extraction, it was not possible to identify age-specific population mortality rates, and thus population estimates are treated as constant to age twenty-one. In addition, the NSW Registry of Births Deaths and Marriages was unable to provide population data disaggregated by Indigenous status. Instead, where Indigenous population estimates are used as the denominator, these have been calculated using the Australian Bureau of Statistics Indigenous population projections (ABS 2019).

Limitations

A more detailed and comprehensive discussion of the limitations of this study are provided in the Conclusion section. However, readers are to be reminded that when interpreting these results, mortality rates have not been used to adjust the population estimates. As a consequence, the age-specific rates of offending presented herein are likely to be conservative. We have no reason to believe that the age-specific rate of mortality was considerably different between the 1984 and 1994 cohorts, so to whatever degree there is underestimation of prevalence, this source of error is likely to affect both cohorts equally. Also, these data do not discount the base population denominator for individuals who move inter-state or overseas. Australia does not have a national criminal justice or police offense recording system and so criminal trajectory analyses are limited to estimates derived from a single jurisdiction. Again, these effects are assumed to be small and equal between the two cohorts. Finally, the crime data used in this study are for recorded offenses only. Therefore, conclusions can only be drawn about crime that is detected and offenses for which there was an official outcome. For reasons described in the Conclusion, we believe this might help to explain some of the significant outcomes of this study.

4 Prevalence

One of the least contentious issues in contemporary criminology is the functional relationship between age and crime – represented as the population prevalence of offending at each age. So ubiquitous is the age-crime curve that criminologists have, over several decades, described its inverted j-shape as one of criminology's only universal findings – a "brute fact" about crime that seems to have been replicated across multiple time periods and in almost all corners of the world (Hirschi & Gottfredson, 1983). Rising slowly at first, the age crime curve typically depicts a relatively low prevalence of criminal offending at the youngest ages of criminal responsibility. By the early teens, population prevalence of offending begins to increase steadily, each year higher than the last, until some point in early adulthood (usually the early twenties) when the relative prevalence of criminal offending begins its long (and less rapid) decline. By forty years of age, the prevalence of offending in any population cohort is often equal to or lower than it was in the early teenage years and by this point only a small proportion of the population is recorded as actively engaged in crime.

With respect to the 1984 and 1994 birth cohorts examined in this study, the same apparent shape appears, with population prevalence increasing (relatively) rapidly between the ages of thirteen and nineteen years, then falling back modestly during the twentieth year (Figure 1). The largest year-on-year increase for both cohorts was between thirteen and fourteen years of age, while the downward shift between the ages of nineteen and twenty was proportionally the same at negative 5 percent. The core functional features of the age-crime curve in both cohorts appear remarkably consistent despite there being some seemingly dramatic shifts in the actual prevalence of criminal offending within the 1994 cohort. For example, the peak age of offending was nineteen years for both cohorts, yet the peak prevalence of offending was almost 50 percent lower (3.8% vs. 2.1%) for those born in 1994. The difference in prevalence between the 1984 and 1994 cohorts first emerges at age fourteen (0.9% vs. 0.6%) and slowly increases throughout adolescence. In cumulative terms (see Figure 2), this year-on-year difference compounds such that by age twenty, the overall population prevalence of offending was almost 50 percent lower among those born in 1994 (9.5% vs. 4.8%). The only apparent similarity between the cohorts was in the prevalence of early onset offending. For both cohorts, the cumulative population prevalence up to and including age thirteen was 0.4 percent.

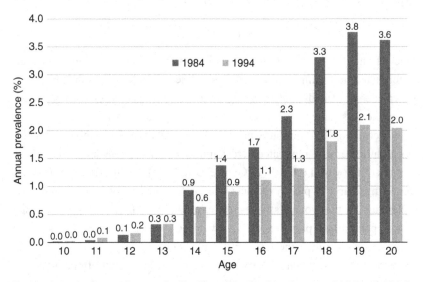

Figure 1 Annual prevalence of offending (% of cohort by age, 1984 and 1994)
Source: Payne et al. (2016) – *Trajectories of two NSW Birth Cohorts [Computer File]*

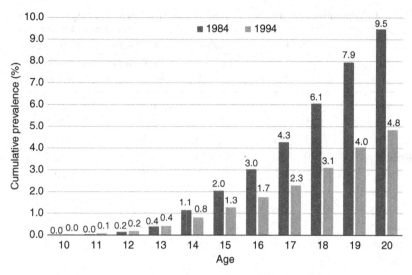

Figure 2 Cumulative prevalence of offending (cumulative % of cohort by age, 1984 and 1994)

Source: Payne et al. (2016) – *Trajectories of two NSW Birth Cohorts [Computer File]*

The almost 50 percent decline in the cumulative prevalence of offending between 1984 and 1994 reflects overall contact with the criminal justice system and suggests that, relative to their 1984-born peers, a very sizable proportion of young people born in 1994 did not have contact with the criminal justice system. However, these aggregate results mask a number of important differences by crime type (Table 1). For example, the population of prevalence of property offending was 56 percent lower among those born in 1994, with vehicle and other property thefts being the two subcategories of property crime with the greatest decline (both down by 59%). Violent offending, although less prevalent than property crime in both cohorts, did not decline by the same magnitude as property crime (down 32%). Specifically, assault and other violent offenses (not including sex offenses and robbery) declined by a relatively modest amount: 28 and 26 percent, respectively. The only crime type for which there was an increase in prevalence between 1984 and 1994 were those offenses classified as breaches or offenses against justice orders. Although a comparatively infrequent crime type, the prevalence of breach offending increased from 0.7 percent in 1984 to 1.0 percent in 1994, an increase of 43 percent.

This comparative analysis of both annual and cumulative prevalence provides some early and important insights into the Australian crime-drop. First, these data confirm that crime has declined, in large part, because of a dramatic

Elements in Criminology

Table 1 Cumulative prevalence of offending to 21 years of age (1984 and 1994)

	1984		1994		Summary of change	
					% difference in prevalence	% change in prevalence
	n	%	n	%		
Violent	2,162	2.6	1,571	1.8	−0.8	−32.3
Assault	975	1.2	748	0.8	−0.3	−28.5
Sex	67	0.1	42	0.0	0.0	−41.6
Robbery	319	0.4	196	0.2	−0.2	−42.7
Other violent	1,459	1.8	1,152	1.3	−0.5	−26.4
Property	3,207	3.8	1,512	1.7	−2.2	−56.0
Burglary	1,030	1.2	594	0.7	−0.6	−46.2
Vehicle theft	830	1.0	363	0.4	−0.6	−59.2
Stealing	1,934	2.3	1,028	1.2	−1.2	−50.4
Other property	1,283	1.5	559	0.6	−0.9	−59.4
Drug	1,384	1.7	1,163	1.3	−0.4	−21.7
Drink driving	2,092	2.5	1,135	1.3	−1.2	−49.4
Traffic	2,496	3.0	1,687	1.9	−1.1	−37.0
Disorder	2,748	3.3	1,707	1.9	−1.4	−42.1
Breach	598	0.7	916	1.0	0.3	42.8
Other	935	1.1	709	0.8	−0.3	−29.3
All	7,900	9.5	4,341	4.9	−4.6	−48.8
All (excl. breaches)	7,887	9.5	4,332	4.8	−4.6	−48.8

Note: Each 'n' represents the total number of unique offenders recorded or each offense. A single offender can appear only once per crime type, but more than once across different crime types.

Source: Payne et al. (2016) – *Trajectories of two NSW Birth Cohorts [Computer File]*

shift in the population prevalence of offending within emerging cohorts of young Australians. Put simply, substantially fewer young people are now coming into contact with the criminal justice system, resulting in substantially fewer recorded crimes committed by younger generations of Australians. Second, that the decline in the prevalence of offending was not the same for all offense types is an interesting artifact of these data and points to some potential causes for this dramatic generational shift. Property offending, for example, was the hardest hit, but is the crime type that is most amenable to the benefits of physical and technical advances in target hardening and securitization. The increased preponderance of target-hardening strategies, including CCTV and other surveillance technologies, have not only made it harder for young offenders to commit crime, but also increased the risks of apprehension and sanction. The significant reduction in vehicle theft, in particular, has been widely attributed to the implementation of various target-hardening and theft-prevention strategies (see Farrell & Brown, 2016), such as the installation of vehicle immobilizers and car alarms. Similar technologies, including bio-technologies, have been introduced into popular consumer electrical products such as mobile phones and personal computers, making these once easy-to-steal and easy-to-sell products much more difficult to convert for personal use or sell for cash on the black market.[10] The personal and financial gains of contemporary property crime are undoubtedly lower and the risks of apprehension higher – fundamental shifts that could realistically have contributed to the disproportional fall in the prevalence of property offending among younger generations of Australians.

5 Frequency and Chronicity

The relationship between age and crime is a function of both prevalence and frequency of offending. The total quantum of offenses committed is a function of both the number of active offenders and the number of crimes those active offenders commit each year (Blumstein et al., 1986). At present, the crime-drop in NSW is understood as a decline in the total volume of crime committed and has yet to parse the joint contribution of both the decline in prevalence (as seen in Section 4) and a potential decline in the rate of offending among active offenders. Figure 3 presents the standardized annual and cumulative rates of offending (per 100,000) for the 1984 and 1994 cohorts. Consistent with the decline in prevalence, the total volume of crime committed by the 1994 cohort was also substantially lower. At the age of peak offending, for example, the standardized rate of offending by the 1994 cohort was down by 36 percent (8,480 vs. 5,421) and, in cumulative terms (see Table 2), the total quantum of crime committed by age twenty-one was down by 31 percent (45,118 vs. 30,937). It is notable that the decline in cumulative prevalence seen in Section 4 – a decline of almost 50 percent – was considerably larger than the decline in the total quantum of crime committed.

---

[10] In an interesting study in the United States, Orrick and Piquero (2015) examined the extent to which cell phones were associated with lower crime in the 1990s and 2000s. They found a significant, negative relationship between changes in cell phone ownership rates and property crime, but little relationship to violent crime.

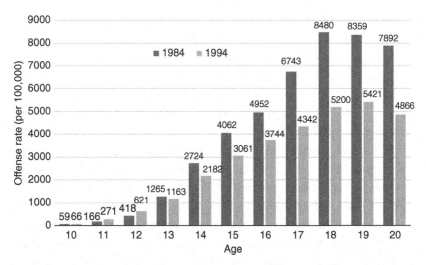

Figure 3 Annual frequency of offending (rate per 100,000 by age, 1984 and 1994)

Note: To equalize the comparison, these offense rates have been standardized to a rate per 100,000 head of population in each cohort. The actual offense rates are lower.

Source: Payne et al. (2016) – *Trajectories of two NSW Birth Cohorts [Computer File]*

The average rate of offending, calculated by dividing total number of crimes by the total number of active offenders, shows an interesting trend. For example, in the 1984 birth cohort the average offending rate was 4.8 offenses whereas for the 1994 birth cohort, the average offending rate was 6.4 offenses. In other words, for those who did come into contact with the criminal justice system, the average number of offenses committed was actually higher, by 34 percent, for the 1994 birth cohort. So, while it is true that the total number of active offenders and the total volume of crime committed by the 1994 birth cohort was lower than for their 1984 peers, that actual number of crimes committed per active offender increased. This suggests that the change between 1984 and 1994 has been driven by the disproportionate disappearance (from official records) of very low rate or infrequent offenders and potentially additional criminal justice actions. What remains in the 1994 cohort is a seemingly more concentrated group of young offenders who appear more frequent in their offending.

By offense type (Table 2), the volume of crime dropped across all categories with the exception of breach and justice related offenses. The largest decline was for property and drink driving offenses (both down by 52%). Of the property crimes, motor vehicle theft experienced the largest decline, down by 63 percent. Violent crimes (–23%), drug crimes (–22%), and disorderly conduct offenses (–28%) were also less frequent in the 1994 cohort, although these

Table 2 Cumulative offense counts to 21 years of age (1984 and 1994)

	1984			1994			Summary of change	
	n	rate (per 100,000)	Average per offender	n	rate (per 100,000)	Average per offender	% change in rate	% change in average per offender
Violent	5,076	6,091.6	2.3	4,211	4,711.7	2.7	-22.7	14.2
Assault	1,549	1,858.9	1.6	1,278	1,430	1.7	-23.1	7.5
Sex	156	187.2	2.3	71	79.4	1.7	-57.6	-27.4
Robbery	585	702	1.8	350	391.6	1.8	-44.2	-2.6
Other violent	2,786	3,343.4	1.9	2,512	2,810.7	2.2	-15.9	14.2
Property	11,693	14,032.5	3.6	6,017	6,732.5	4.0	-52.0	9.1
Burglary	2,748	3,297.8	2.7	1,577	1,764.5	2.7	-46.5	0.0
Vehicle theft	1,712	2,054.5	2.1	686	767.6	1.9	-62.6	-8.4
Stealing	4,346	5,215.5	2.2	2,511	2,809.6	2.4	46.1	8.7
Other property	2,887	3,464.6	2.3	1,243	1,390.8	2.2	-59.9	-1.2
Drug	2,239	2,687	1.6	1,869	2,091.2	1.6	-22.2	0.0
Drink driving	2,388	2,865.8	1.1	1,227	1,372.9	1.1	-52.1	0.0
Traffic	5,982	7,178.9	2.4	3,984	4,457.7	2.4	-37.9	-1.5
Disorder	6,817	8,180.9	2.5	5,246	5,869.8	3.1	-28.3	23.9
Breach	1326	1,591.3	2.2	3,848	4,305.6	4.2	170.6	89.5
Other	1411	1,693.3	1.5	1,243	1,390.8	1.8	-17.9	16.2
All	37,596	45,118.1	4.8	27,649	30,936.6	6.4	-31.4	33.8
All (excl. breaches)	36,270	43,526.8	4.6	23,801	26,631.1	5.5	-38.8	19.5

Source: Payne et al. (2016) – *Trajectories of two NSW Birth Cohorts [Computer File]*

figures are, perhaps, confounded by the fall in prevalence and the disproportionate disappearance of infrequent offenders. As noted, for all crimes combined, the decline in prevalence was greater than the decline in frequency, meaning that the average offense rate per active offender was, in fact, higher in 1994 cohort. This trend was consistent for the majority of offenses, such as assault and other violent offending, stealing, disorderly conduct offenses, and breach offenses. For other offense types, however, the average number of offenses committed by active offenders either declined (this was the case for sex offenses, robbery, and motor vehicle theft) or remained unchanged (such as for burglary, drug offenses, drink driving, and traffic offenses).

By age, there is a notable trend (see Figure 4). At the earliest ages (age ten and eleven), the offense rate for active offenders was higher for the 1984 cohort (4.1 and 4.5 offenses, respectively) than for the 1994 cohort (2.7 and 3.4 offenses, respectively). This trend shifts for almost all ages after and including age twelve, where the average rate of offending was higher for the 1994 cohort.

The underlying story of these data so far is that the crime-drop in NSW is likely to have been the consequence of a generational fall in participation (prevalence) but not a population-wide shift in the actual frequency of offending among active offenders. To explore this further, Table 3 classifies the offenders in each cohort according to the number of crimes they had committed before their twenty-first birthday. We use three categories: those who committed one offense only, those who committed between two and four offenses, and those

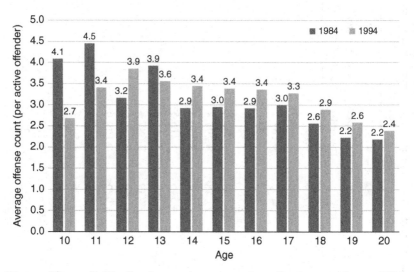

Figure 4 Rate of offending by age (rate per active offender at each age, 1984 and 1994)

Source: Payne et al. (2016) – *Trajectories of two NSW Birth Cohorts [Computer File]*

who committed five or more offenses. This categorization is common in criminal career research (Tracy et al., 1990). For each group, Table 3 also provides the number of offenses recoded as well as a series of summary data about the relative prevalence of each group.

The single largest category of offenders in both the 1984 and 1994 cohorts committed just one offense (Table 3). In the 1984 cohort, these once-only offenders represented 4 percent of the total birth cohort and 41 percent of active offenders. Their offenses represented just 9 percent of all the offenses recorded for the cohort. Compare this with the 1,529 once-only offenders in the 1994 cohort. Together, they represented a little under 2 percent (1.7%) of the total birth cohort and 35 percent of the offender cohort. Their offenses represented approximately 6 percent of all the crimes committed by their cohort. The population prevalence of once-only offending halved between 1984 and 1994, and these offenders now represent a smaller proportion of the total offender pool and they are responsible for a lower proportion of the overall offense count.

The population prevalence of moderate offending (two to four offenses) also declined between 1984 and 1994 (3.4%, down to 1.6%) and, consequently, moderate offenders were also responsible for a lower proportion of the overall offending within their cohorts (23.4%, down to 16.4%). This proportional decline in offenses attributable to moderate offenders is driven partly by the fall in prevalence, but also a downward shift in the average number of offenses committed (3.0 offenses, down to 2.7). The prevalence of chronic offending (five or more offenses) also declined between 1984 and 1994 (2.2%, down to 1.5%), however, chronic offenders now represented a larger proportion of the active offender pool (23.1%, up to 31.5%) and a larger share of the total volume of crime (67.8%, up to 77.2%) despite that their rate of offending remained unchanged (13.5 offenses per chronic offender).

Table 4 explores in more detail the changing offense patterns and profiles of those who by twenty-one years of age were classified as chronic offenders. For violent offending, the average offending rate increased from 1.9 to 2.5 offenses per offender, and the proportion of chronic offenders charged with at least one violent offense increased from 62 percent to 71 percent. Chronic offenders were consequently responsible for a larger share of all violent offending committed by the 1994 cohort (81%, up from 70%). The increase in violence was largely driven by offenses classified as "other violence," which excludes assault, sex offenses, and robbery, but includes weapons-related offenses, threatening behavior, stalking, and other interpersonal offending. Property offending declined among chronic offenders from an average of 5.0 offenses in 1984 to 3.9 offenses in 1994. This decline was evidenced across all subcategories of property

Table 3 Once-only, moderate, and chronic offenders (1984 and 1994)

	Offenders (n)	Offenses (n)	% of population	% of offenders	Average offenses	% of offenses
1984						
Once-only	3,216	3,216	3.9	40.8	1	8.9
2–4 offenses	2,853	8,480	3.4	36.2	3.0	23.4
5+ offenses	1,818	24,574	2.2	23.1	13.5	67.8
Total	7,887	36,270	9.5	100	4.6	100
1994						
Once-only	1,529	1,529	1.7	35.3	1	6.4
2–4 offenses	1,438	3,892	1.6	33.2	2.7	16.4
5+ offenses	1,365	18,380	1.5	31.5	13.5	77.2
Total	4,332	23,801	4.8	100	5.5	100

Source: Payne et al. (2016) – *Trajectories of two NSW Birth Cohorts [Computer File]*

Table 4 Average offense rate and proportion of offenses committed by chronic offenders (5+) (1984 and 1994)

	1984				1994			
	Offense count (n)	Average offense count per chronic offender	% of chronics with at least one count	% of all offenses attributable to chronics	Offense count (n)	Average offense count per chronic offender	% of chronics with at least one count	% of all offenses attributable to chronics
Violent	3,545	1.9	61.6	69.8	3,415	2.5	71.2	81.1
Assault	1,123	0.6	32.9	72.5	1,030	0.8	38.8	80.6
Sex	57	0.0	1.6	36.5	44	0.0	1.6	62.0
Robbery	434	0.2	11.9	74.2	317	0.2	12.2	90.6
Other violent	1,931	1.1	46.6	69.3	2,024	1.5	56.1	80.6
Property	9,022	5.0	80.7	77.2	5,334	3.9	74.4	88.6
Burglary	2,361	1.3	38.9	85.9	1,444	1.1	35.2	91.6
Vehicle theft	1,446	0.8	32.2	84.5	625	0.5	22.3	91.1
Stealing	3,246	1.8	57.8	74.7	2,170	1.6	55.2	86.4
Other property	1,969	1.1	40.0	68.2	1,095	0.8	32.2	88.1
Drug	1,224	0.7	35.4	54.7	1,080	0.8	41.0	57.8
Drink driving	570	0.3	23.2	23.9	309	0.2	19.3	25.2

Table 4 (cont.)

	1984				1994			
	Offense count (n)	Average offense count per chronic offender	% of chronics with at least one count	% of all offenses attributable to chronics	Offense count (n)	Average offense count per chronic offender	% of chronics with at least one count	% of all offenses attributable to chronics
Traffic	3,823	2.1	54.7	63.9	2,672	2.0	54.0	67.1
Disorder	5,005	2.8	74.1	73.4	4,500	3.3	80.3	85.8
Breach	1,151	0.6	25.9	86.8	3,549	2.6	52.0	92.2
Other	1,032	0.6	33.8	73.1	1,066	0.8	39.9	85.8
All	25,725	14.2	100.0	68.4	21,929	16.1	100.0	79.3
All (excl. breaches)	24,574	13.5	100.0	67.8	18,380	13.5	100.0	77.2

Source: Payne et al. (2016) – *Trajectories of two NSW Birth Cohorts [Computer File]*

offending, however, in most cases the proportion of chronic offenders having committed at least one crime in those categories remained relatively consistent. The exception was for motor vehicle theft, of which only 22 percent of chronic offenders in 1994 were arrested, down from 32 percent in 1984. Drug, drink driving, and traffic offenses remained relatively unchanged between the two cohorts, while disorderly conduct and breach offenses increased.

Perhaps the most notable of findings from the chronic offender analysis is how, despite these changes, chronic offenders become disproportionately responsible for a larger share of most offending categories. For example, chronic offenders were responsible for 70 percent of all violent offenses committed by the 1984 birth cohort, though this increased to 81 percent within the 1994 cohort. Similarly, property offending increased from 77 percent to 81 percent. For the subcategories of robbery, burglary, and motor vehicle theft, chronic offenders in 1994 were responsible for nine in every ten recorded offenses.

Not surprisingly, the total volume was substantially lower among those young people born in 1994. However, the decline in volume was not as large as was the decline in prevalence. This suggests that the crime-drop in NSW was disproportionally driven by a change in the total number of people coming into contact with the criminal justice system, and that the "disappearance" was disproportionally greater among those who would have had only limited contact with the police (i.e., one offense). Consequently, the rate of active offending appears greater in the 1994 cohort, but probably only because the denominator (active offenders) has concentrated to the more frequent end of the offending spectrum.

The inequality of these data by age and offense type provides important insight into the potential causes of the crime-drop in NSW. For some offenses, mostly acquisitive offenses such as burglary, robbery, and motor vehicle theft, even active offenders were committing fewer offenses. This suggests that these offenses are either less rewarding or harder to commit such that even those who engage in that type of offending are doing so less often. By age, the lower rate of offending at ages ten and eleven suggest that even the earliest onset offenders were committing less crime in 1994, or were being detected, charged, and processed for fewer offenses. This trend changes from twelve years of age onward. In our view, this changing age profile is likely to reflect the broader shift to the more systematic use of cautioning and diversion that should have muted the offense rate of early onset offenders, and then later prevented (disproportionally) the entry of low rate or once-only offenders into the criminal justice system.

6 Onset

The age at which an offender first has contact with the criminal justice system has long been recognized as an important criminal career parameter (Blumstein et al., 1986; Piquero et al., 2003). Onset ages, for example, help to delineate early onset from adolescent- and late-onset offending – three time points that have been shown to link to particular patterns of offending over the life-course. Early onset offending, for example, typically foreshadows a more chronic offending career that is higher in volume and longer in length (Piquero et al., 2003). Adolescent-onset offending, on the other hand, is typically linked to a relatively short criminal career of relatively fewer crimes.

In the context of the NSW crime-drop, there appears to have been little impact on the population prevalence of early onset offending. In the 1984 cohort, for example, there were 129 children who had contact with the police between the ages of ten and twelve years (Table 5). They represented just 0.2 percent of the population born in that year. For the 1994 cohort, there were 166 early onset offenders who similarly represented 0.2 percent of the population born in 1994. What differs between the cohorts in terms of early onset offending is not their population prevalence, but their relative prevalence within the overall offending cohort, increasing from 1.6 percent in 1984 to 3.8 percent in 1994. For adolescent-limited offending, the trend was reversed, with the population prevalence declining by almost half (4.1% down to 2.1%), while the relative prevalence of adolescent-onset offending remained unchanged (43.4%, respectively). Finally, for adult-onset offending the popula-tion prevalence fell by 50 percent (5.2%, down to 2.6%), but the relative prevalence within the offending cohort remained relatively unchanged (55.0% and 52.7%, respectively).

Overall, these data translate into a modest downward shift in the average age of onset between the 1984 and 1994 birth cohorts (Table 5). For all offenders born in 1984, the average age of first contact with the criminal justice system was 17.3 years. By 1994, this fell by a little over two months to 17.1 years. The median age of onset for both cohorts was unchanged at eighteen years, however, this cohort-level comparative analysis is confounded by the significant and disproportionate decline in participation, particularly in the less frequent and later-onset offending categories. Consequently, although it might *appear* as if the 1994 birth cohort had started offending at an earlier age, this result is not (as we have seen earlier) the consequence of a growth in early onset offending, but rather a disproportionate decline in the prevalence of adolescent- and adult-onset offending.

To explore this in more detail, Table 6 presents the average onset ages of three categories of offenders: once-only offenders, moderate offenders, and chronic

Table 5 Age of onset categories (1984 and 1994)

	1984			1994		
	Offenders (n)	% of offenders	% of population	Offenders (n)	% of offenders	% of population
Early (10–12 years)	129	1.6	0.2	166	3.8	0.2
Adolescent (13–17 years)	3,429	43.4	4.1	1,882	43.4	2.1
Adult (18–20 years)	4,342	55.0	5.2	2,284	52.7	2.6
Total	7,900	100.0	9.5	4,332	100.0	4.8

Source: Payne et al. (2016) – *Trajectories of two NSW Birth Cohorts [Computer File]*

Table 6 Age of onset by categories of chronicity (1984 and 1994)

	1984				1994			
	Min	Max	Mean	Median	Min	Max	Mean	Median
Once-only	10	20	18.4	19	12	20	18.8	19
2–4 offenses	11	20	17.3	18	10	20	17.3	18
5+ offenses	10	20	15.6	15	10	20	15.0	15
Total	10	20	17.3	18	10	20	17.1	18

Source: Payne et al. (2016) – *Trajectories of two NSW Birth Cohorts [Computer File]*

offenders. Although this does not fully account for the fall in participation across these groups, it nevertheless compares the onset of offending among conceptually similar types of offenders, groups for which we might expect a shift in average onset if there has been some systematic cause. Once-only offenders in the 1984 birth cohort first had contact with the police at 18.4 years of age. The youngest was ten years old, the oldest was twenty, and the median age was nineteen years. Contrast this to the 1994 birth cohort where the average age of onset for once-only offending was fractionally higher at 18.8 years. The youngest once-only offender was twelve, the oldest was twenty, and the median was unchanged at nineteen years. Moderate offending started at an average age of 17.3 years (median 18) and this was the same for both the 1984 and 1994 birth cohorts. For chronic offending, the average age of onset declined modestly, falling from an average age of 15.6 years in the 1984 cohort to 15.0 years in the

1994 cohort. Overall, these data do not point to some single unidirectional change in the onset of offending throughout the early phases of the NSW crime-drop. Instead, the average age of once-only offending increased, most likely because once-only offending was disproportionately "prevented" in the younger age groups or because once-only offending was systematically delayed. The reverse is true for chronic offenders who, during the crime-drop, actually started offending at an earlier age.

It is difficult to understand why this might have occurred, although there are several possible explanations. First, chronic offending is likely a consequence of two processes. For some young kids, the propensity to crime is rooted in early childhood experiences and is manifested as early behavioral and conduct problems in the home and school – all of which predate officially recorded offenses. Relative to their peers, the antisocial conduct of these soon-to-be chronic offenders is frequent and overt, and attracts attention from authority, both in school and on the streets. This antisocial behavior may appear more obvious and overt, not because the offending is any more serious than a decade earlier, but because there is now a larger proportion of adolescent-onset and once-only offenders who are no longer coming into contact with the criminal justice system. The decline in the average age of onset might reflect an increase in risk of detection, rather than any systematic change in the propensity of these young children to start committing crime at earlier ages. For other young kids, chronic offending might be a consequence of accumulated disadvantage, especially the negative and long-term consequences of criminal justice sanction. To prevent this, formal cautioning and diversion has become a core pillar of the Australian criminal justice system and there is an increasing imperative to divert young first-time or low-level offenders away from the criminal justice system. For the majority of young offenders, this seems to have had no real benefit in reducing longer-term contact with the criminal justice system (see Payne, Kwaitkowski & Wundersitz, 2008), but has formalized a previously informal process for documenting the offending of young people. A key criticism of diversion is its potential to net-widen the reach of the criminal justice system, capturing people (young and disadvantaged) who might have previously been warned or cautioned without formal diversion. In the United Kingdom, Farrington and Maughan (1999) compared two London-based birth cohorts born in 1953 and 1960. The cautioning of young offenders (age ten to sixteen) was introduced in about 1970 and appeared only to affect the younger of the two cohorts. Importantly, however, the proportion of young people ever convicted was the same for both cohorts, but an additional 4 percent of the younger cohort were cautioned. The authors concluded cautioning had not so much "diverted" young offenders but rather widened the net of recorded offenders. For chronic offenders in this current study, the fall in the average age of onset might reflect this broader shift to formalize early contact under the guise of diversion and early intervention.

Where at an aggregate level there have been only modest changes in the average age of onset, at the offense level there have been some stark shifts between the two birth cohorts. Table 7 provides the distribution of offenses at first contact with the criminal justice system. In the 1984 offender cohort, property crimes were the most probable first offense. One in three (32.4%) members of that cohort started their criminal careers with a property offense, most likely a stealing or low-level theft offense (16.7%). For the 1994 cohort, property offending was much less likely to be the onset offense (down to 25.3%) and was now equal in prevalence to disorderly conduct offenses. Within the property-offending category, the relative decline was greatest for motor vehicle theft (down 44%) and within the category of violent offending, the only offense type that was less likely to be an offender's first offense was robbery (down 11%).

Table 7 Offense type at age of onset (1984 and 1994)

	1984 (n=7887)		1994 (n=4332)		Summary	
	n	%	n	%	% difference	% change
Violent	1,293	16.4	909	21.0	4.6	28.0
Assault	429	5.4	293	6.8	1.3	24.3
Sex	42	0.5	25	0.6	0.0	8.4
Robbery	149	1.9	73	1.7	−0.2	−10.8
Other violent	790	10.0	591	13.6	3.6	36.2
Property	2,552	32.4	1,098	25.3	−7.0	−21.7
Burglary	591	7.5	321	7.4	−0.1	−1.1
Vehicle theft	479	6.1	147	3.4	−2.7	−44.1
Stealing	1,318	16.7	625	14.4	−2.3	−13.7
Other property	677	8.6	221	5.1	−3.5	−40.6
Drug	777	9.9	589	13.6	3.7	38.0
Drink driving	1,478	18.7	759	17.5	−1.2	−6.5
Traffic	1,543	19.6	946	21.8	2.3	11.6
Disorder	1,758	22.3	1,−096	25.3	3.0	13.5
Breach	133	1.7	288	6.6	5.0	294.2
Other	379	4.8	219	5.1	0.3	5.2

Note: *Double counting permitted if an offender was processed for two different offenses at the same age*

Source: Payne et al. (2016) – *Trajectories of two NSW Birth Cohorts [Computer File]*

7 Trajectories

To this point, our efforts to understand the NSW crime-drop has focused on the comparative analysis of differences between the two birth cohorts with respect to the individual criminal career parameters of participation, frequency, and onset. The story has been somewhat complex, since changes in one parameter confound the interpretation of changes in another – a challenge long acknowledged by both the proponents (Blumstein et al., 1986) and the critics (Gottfredson & Hirschi, 1986) of the criminal career paradigm. To answer this challenge, and indeed the challenge set by the developmental typologies of Moffitt (1993), Nagin and Land (1993) introduced a semi-parametric group-based trajectory modelling (SPGM) technique to capture and partition the apparent heterogeneity of individual criminal activity into a set of seemingly homogenous groups of offenders who follow (roughly) the same trajectory into and out of crime over time. SPGM is best understood as a data-reduction technique, much like latent class or cluster analysis, which looks to produce "averaged" representations of patterns and structures within data that at the individual level is both complete and highly heterogeneous. The technique has been a popular method for the study of life-course offending trajectories (Jennings & Reingle, 2012; Piquero, 2008) and has inspired a generation of research studies on the developmental shape of criminal careers. Perhaps its greatest achievement was to show that the aggregate age-crime curve was not unimodal at the individual level, as Gottfredson and Hirschi (1990) argued, but rather a composite of different trajectory shapes and sizes that would otherwise be hidden in the simple presentation of aggregate age-crime calculations. Moreover, various risk factors have also been found to distinguish between the different offender trajectories.[11]

For comparative purposes, we estimate an SPGM model for each of the two birth cohorts separately. We limit our search to the parameterization of four latent structures and we compare the quantitative and qualitative structures of these trajectories with respect to the average timing of onset, the timing and speed of escalation, the timing and frequency of peak offending, and the timing of desistance (or the move to desistance, given that our data are censored at twenty-one years of age). We estimate the four latent trajectories using a zero-inflated Poisson model and a quadratic functional form for each trajectory. The

---

[11] Critics argue that SPGM produces an oversimplified representation of criminal trajectory complexity and encourages an atheoretical overreliance on simplified data structures that do not represent "real groups" or that risk the reification of "groups" into selective criminal justice policies that have the potential to do more harm. Nevertheless, in the present analysis, SPGM offers a unique window into the totality of change between the 1984 and 1994 cohorts, by taking into account patterns of homogeneity across multiple criminal career parameters.

SPGM analyses presented here has been operationalized using the *traj* module designed by Jones and Nagin (2013) for implementation in Stata (Statacorp 2017).

The modelling outcomes for both the 1984 and 1994 cohorts are provided in Table 8, while the graphical representation of these models is presented in Figures 5 and 6. In both models, the SPGM generalized to four almost-identical trajectories. Herein, we describe these trajectories as "Early onset, High-rate (EH)," "Adolescent-onset, Limited (AL)," "Late Adolescent-onset, Moderate (LAM)," and "Once-only, Low-rate" (OL)." There is, of course, a fifth group in both birth cohorts that is not estimated in these models – those who committed no offenses at all. These young people represent 90 percent and 95 percent of the cohorts, respectively, and are an important reference group against which the population prevalence of the four SPGM-derived trajectories can be calculated.

In both cohorts, the single largest (by membership size) offending group were those who committed just once offense before the age of twenty-one. For the 1984 cohort, this OL group represented 78 percent of the total offending cohort, or 7.6 percent of the total 1984 birth cohort. This contrasts to an OL membership size of 73 percent in the 1994 offender cohort (3.3 percent of the total population born in 1994). This result is broadly consistent with the evidence presented earlier and confirms that there was a substantial and disproportional drop in the prevalence of once-only or very low rate offending.

The next largest trajectory in terms of membership or group size was those offenders who started offending in early adolescence (at about the age of thirteen or fourteen) and committed between two and four offenses over a three- to four-year period before then disappearing from the criminal justice system. These AL offenders represented almost 10 percent of the 1984 offending cohort and this translated to 0.9 percent of the total birth cohort. Among their peers born in 1994, membership to the AL offending group was higher at 15 percent or 0.7 percent of the total 1994 birth cohort. In terms of trajectory shape, the differences are modest. For example, the peak rate of AL offending occurs for both cohorts at sixteen years of age and the estimated peak offense rate is roughly equal for both cohorts (1.9 offenses vs. 1.8 offenses). Thus, while AL offending has become proportionally more prevalent during the crime decline, the average frequency of within-trajectory offending has remained mostly unchanged between the cohorts.

Late-adolescent onset offending represented approximately 9 percent of the 1984 offending cohort and 9 percent of the 1994 offending cohort. In population terms, this late-starting moderate-rate offending group is 56 percent less prevalent among those born in 1994 (0.4%) than those born in 1984 (0.9%). Of the

Table 8 Four-trajectory GBTM solution (ZIP: 2,2,2,2), offenders born in 1984 and 1994

		1984				1994			
		Estimate	S.E.	T	P	Estimate	S.E.	T	P
Once-only Low-rate (OL)	Intercept	-8.72	0.20	-44.53	0.00	-10.21	0.35	-29.00	0.00
	Linear	1.37	0.05	30.00	0.00	1.66	0.08	20.82	0.00
	Quadratic	-0.06	0.00	-21.34	0.00	-0.07	0.00	-15.32	0.00
Adolescent-onset Limited (AL)	Intercept	-8.06	0.21	-38.32	0.00	-6.95	0.19	-36.91	0.00
	Linear	2.48	0.06	39.32	0.00	2.11	0.06	37.49	0.00
	Quadratic	-0.18	0.00	-36.83	0.00	-0.15	0.00	-35.47	0.00
Late-onset Moderate (LAM)	Intercept	-12.75	0.44	-28.95	0.00	-8.72	0.29	-29.66	0.00
	Linear	2.78	0.10	28.75	0.00	2.14	0.07	29.88	0.00
	Quadratic	-0.14	0.01	-25.82	0.00	-0.11	0.00	-25.99	0.00
Early onset High-rate (EH)	Intercept	-3.13	0.10	-32.74	0.00	-1.15	0.08	-13.68	0.00
	Linear	1.35	0.03	49.27	0.00	0.90	0.03	35.34	0.00
	Quadratic	-0.09	0.00	-45.92	0.00	-0.07	0.00	-34.95	0.00
Trajectory assignment probabilities									
OL	(%)	77.88	0.57	137.16	0.00	72.84	0.78	93.61	0.00
AL	(%)	9.18	0.43	21.47	0.00	14.83	0.67	22.21	0.00
LAM	(%)	9.10	0.39	23.21	0.00	8.61	0.48	17.88	0.00

EH	(%)	3.84	0.23	16.84	0.00	3.72	0.30	12.44	0.00

Model Diagnostics

BIC	(N=86,900)	−65,428.28				(N=47,751)	−42,828.45		
BIC	(N=7,900)	−65,140.30				(N=4,341)	−42,810.47		
AIC		−65,357.99					−42,762.65		
L		−65,342.99					−42,747.65		

Source: Payne et al. (2016) – *Trajectories of two NSW Birth Cohorts [Computer File]*

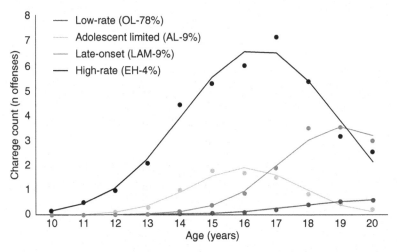

Figure 5 Four-trajectory solution (ZIP: 2,2,2,2) for offenders born in 1984
Source: Payne et al. (2016) – *Trajectories of two NSW Birth Cohorts [Computer File]*

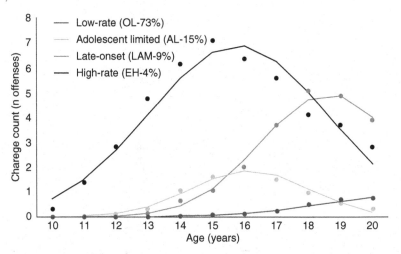

Figure 6 Four-trajectory solution (ZIP: 2,2,2,2) for offenders born in 1994
Source: Payne et al. (2016) – *Trajectories of two NSW Birth Cohorts [Computer File]*

trajectories estimated in these two full models, it was in this LAM group where the most significant changes in trajectory shape were observed. For example, in 1984, LAM offending is estimated to have commenced at between sixteen and seventeen years of age, whereas the estimated age at first offense was between fourteen and fifteen years for these LAM offenders born in 1994. In terms of the frequency of offending, the 1984 cohort hit a peak offending rate of 3.6 offenses per annum at nineteen years of age. For their younger peers, the peak rate of offending was 4.7 offenses at the same age. The result of this is a considerably higher total offense rate for LAM offenders born in 1994 (twenty-one offenses) than those born in 1984 (thirteen offenses).

The final trajectory (EH) was the smallest in size for both cohorts, but disproportionately responsible for a large share of the total offenses committed by each cohort. Starting their criminal careers at an average age of eleven, these EH offenders typically escalated to peak offending within five years. They comprised 3.8 percent of the offender population born in 1984 and 3.7 percent of the offenders born in 1994. Of their respective birth cohorts, EH offenders represented 0.4 and 0.2 percent, respectively. However, while EH offending appears half as prevalent in the 1994 cohort, the estimated total number of offenses committed by EH offenders was higher in this younger group (44 offenses vs. 38 offenses). These data speak to an important trend toward the concentration of more chronic offenders during the crime decline, but not a significant reduction in their offending.

8 Young Women

Developmental and life-course studies of crime have, until recently at least, favored the analysis of male offending patterns and trajectories. The study of young women has been historically limited by smaller sample sizes and methodological approaches that have prioritized the analysis of male offending trajectories (Piquero & Piquero, 2015). More recent efforts have since shed light on the comparative differences between male and female criminal careers, illustrating how these parameters can vary in degree and kind (e.g., Loeber et al., 2017; Piquero, Piquero, & Narvey, in-press). In one recent examination, Loeber et al. (2017) examined female delinquency from childhood to young adulthood using data from the Pittsburgh Youth Study and then compared those results to existing analyses from the Pittsburgh Youth Study of males. Their analyses showed that (1) female prevalence and frequency of offending was lower than males; (2) while onset ages were similar, females desisted quicker; (3) males were more likely to be recidivistic and chronic than females; and (4) trajectory-based analyses revealed similar groups across males and females but females were observed in greater proportions in the non- and low-offending groups (see Loeber et al., 2017).

Importantly, the contextual and causal antecedents of the criminal onset and persistence among young women have been shown to differ from their male peers and these differences might condition the relative strength of any of the exogenous changes that are thought to have precipitated the crime-drop.

Young women in this study comprise a little over half of both the 1984 and 1994 birth cohorts, but within the offending cohort they represented 18 and 19 percent, respectively. To age twenty-one, the cumulative prevalence of criminal justice contact among young women was 3.6 percent for the 1984 cohort and 1.8 percent in the 1994 cohort. Like their male peers, the prevalence of offending among young women halved. Beyond this aggregate similarity, there were a number of notable gender differences within specific crime categories. The prevalence of violent offending, for example, declined for young women, however the extent of the decline was not as large as it was for young men. As a subcategory of violence, the prevalence of assault was actually unchanged between the 1984 and 1994 cohorts (0.4% for both). Property crime dropped for both men and women, although the decline was larger for young women (down 63% from a prevalence of 1.6% to 0.6%) than it was for young men (down 53%).

The average frequency of offending among active offenders increased for young women, a trend that was consistent with the aggregate cohort data presented earlier (Table 9). Young women born in 1984 had committed an average of 3.9 offenses before their twenty-first birthday and this increased to 4.6 offenses for the 1994 cohort. Proportionally, this increase in offending frequency was not as high for young women (up by 18%) as it was for young men (up by 36%) and within specific offending categories the trend by gender was inconsistent. For example, while the prevalence of assault offending remained unchanged for young women, the rate of offending for each assault offender decreased from 1.7 offenses to 1.6 offenses. For young men, the reverse was true in that the rate of assault offending increased (from 1.6 to 1.7 offenses) as the population prevalence of assault offending decreased. The same trend appears for robbery where the prevalence of offending remains unchanged but the average number of robbery offenses committed declined among young women (from 1.6 to 1.1 offenses). For young men, the prevalence of robbery declined while the rate of robbery offending stayed the same (at 1.9 offenses).

With regard to onset and chronicity, we note that the changes experienced by young women were not dissimilar to those of their male counterparts. Proportional to the active offender population in each of the 1984 and 1994 cohorts, there was an increase in the prevalence of early onset offending among young women (from 1.1% to 3.0%). The prevalence of adolescent-onset offending was relatively unchanged among young women (44% and 45%, respectively), but decreased by half as a proportion of the overall population cohort (1.6%, down to 0.8%). The same was true for young men, where adolescent-onset offending remained unchanged as a proportion of the overall offending cohort (43% both years), but decreased considerably as a proportion of the total population (6.3%, down to 3.3%). Finally, the prevalence of adult-onset offending also declined considerably among the young female and young male cohorts.

In terms of chronicity (Table 10), we make a number of observations. First, once-only offending is more prevalent in female offending cohorts (see Piquero

Table 9 Prevalence and frequency, by gender (1984 and 1994)

| | Female | | | | Male | | | |
| | 1984 | | 1994 | | 1984 | | 1994 | |
	Prevalence by age 21 (%)	Rate per active offender	Prevalence by age 21 (%)	Rate per active offender	Prevalence by age 21 (%)	Rate per active offender	Prevalence by age 21 (%)	Rate per active offender
Violent	0.9	2.2	0.7	2.4	4.0	2.4	2.8	2.7
Assault	0.4	1.7	0.4	1.6	1.8	1.6	1.3	1.7
Sex	0.0	0.0	0.0	1.5	0.2	2.3	0.1	1.7
Robbery	0.1	1.6	0.1	1.1	0.6	1.9	0.4	1.9
Other violent	0.7	1.7	0.5	2.0	2.7	2.0	2.0	2.2
Property	1.6	3.3	0.6	3.2	5.7	3.7	2.7	4.2
Burglary	0.3	2.0	0.1	1.8	2.0	2.8	1.2	2.7
SMV	0.3	1.5	0.1	1.5	1.6	2.1	0.7	1.9
Stealing	1.1	2.2	0.5	2.3	3.4	2.3	1.8	2.5
Other property	0.7	3.0	0.2	2.6	2.2	2.0	1.0	2.1
Drug	0.4	1.6	0.3	1.4	2.7	1.6	2.3	1.6

Table 9 (cont.)

	Female				Male			
	1984		1994		1984		1994	
	Prevalence by age 21 (%)	Rate per active offender	Prevalence by age 21 (%)	Rate per active offender	Prevalence by age 21 (%)	Rate per active offender	Prevalence by age 21 (%)	Rate per active offender
Drink	0.8	1.1	0.4	1.0	3.9	1.2	2.0	1.1
Traffic	0.7	1.9	0.6	1.8	4.9	2.5	3.1	2.5
Disorder	0.9	2.1	0.5	2.6	5.3	2.5	3.2	3.2
Breach	0.2	3.0	0.3	3.2	1.2	2.1	1.7	4.4
Other	0.4	1.5	0.3	1.9	1.8	1.5	1.3	1.7
All	3.6	3.9	1.8	4.6	14.5	5.0	7.7	6.8
All (excl. breaches)	3.6	3.7	1.8	4.1	14.4	4.8	7.6	5.8

Source: Payne et al. (2016) – *Trajectories of two NSW Birth Cohorts [Computer File]*

Table 10 Onset and chronicity, by gender (1984 and 1994)

	Female				Male			
	1984		1994		1984		1994	
	% of offenders	% of population	% of offenders	% of population	% of offenders	% of population	% of offenders	% of population
Age of onset								
Early (10–12 years)	1.1	<0.1	3.0	0.1	1.8	0.3	4.3	0.3
Adolescent (13–17 years)	43.7	1.6	45.2	0.8	43.3	6.3	42.9	3.3
Adult (18–20 years)	55.2	2.0	51.8	0.9	54.9	8.0	52.8	4.1
Chronicity								
Once-only	44.1	1.5	42.7	0.8	37.8	5.5	32.8	2.5
2–4 offenses	35.3	1.2	32.0	0.6	35.9	5.2	32.3	2.5
5+ offenses	20.6	0.7	26.4	0.5	26.3	3.8	34.9	2.7

Source: Payne et al. (2016) – *Trajectories of two NSW Birth Cohorts [Computer File]*

et al., 2005) than in male offending cohorts and this trend did not change between 1984 and 1994. Second, for both females and males, the population prevalence of once-only offending declined by more than 50 percent. The same was true for moderate offending of between two and four offenses. The relative prevalence of moderate offending was approximately the same in both the male and female offending cohorts, but the population prevalence of moderate offending fell by half between 1984 and 1994. Finally, chronic offending among young female offenders increased as a proportion of the offending cohort (25%, up from 19%) and this experience was the same for young male offenders. However, as a proportion of the population, the prevalence of chronic offending declined in both the female and male cohorts. Essentially, the relative experience of young women and the changes seen between 1984 and 1994 were not particular or specific to women, but mirrored the experience of young men who were growing up in NSW at the same time. This suggests that whatever the cause of the crime-drop, the experience was not fundamentally gendered, but general and of equal impact regardless of gender.

9 Indigenous Australians

Empirical research has long documented the overrepresentation of Indigenous people in the Australian criminal justice system (Payne & Piquero, 2016; Weatherburn, 2014) and this study is no exception. In both the 1984 and 1994 birth cohorts, young Indigenous people born in NSW were three times as likely to have had contact with the police before age twenty-one (Table 11). In all, 32 percent of Indigenous young people born in 1984 had at least one contact with the police before turning twenty-one. For their non-Indigenous peers, the comparative prevalence was 9 percent. For the 1994 Indigenous-born cohort, the prevalence of contact declined to 14 percent. Proportionally, the decline in prevalence was greater, at 56 percent, for the Indigenous population than for the non-Indigenous population where prevalence declined by 50 precent from 8.6 percent in 1984 to 4.3 percent in 1994.

Consistent with the aggregate results presented earlier, the frequency of offending among active offenders increased for both the Indigenous and non-Indigenous cohorts, although it is important to note that the increase among Indigenous offenders was greater than non-Indigenous offenders. For example, among active indigenous offenders born in 1984, the average number of offenses committed by age twenty-one was twelve. This increased by 39 percent to 16.7 offenses and compares to a more modest increase, in the order 22 percent, among non-Indigenous offenders (from 3.7 to 4.5 offenses).

Table 11 Prevalence and frequency, by Indigenous status (1984 and 1994)

	Indigenous				Non-Indigenous			
	1984		1994		1984		1994	
	Prevalence by age 21 (%)	Rate per active offender	Prevalence by age 21 (%)	Rate per active offender	Prevalence by age 21 (%)	Rate per active offender	Prevalence by age 21 (%)	Rate per active offender
Violent	18.9	3.3	10.4	3.7	1.9	2.0	1.3	2.2
Assault	10.4	2.1	6.2	2.1	0.8	1.3	0.5	1.5
Sex	0.7	2.0	0.2	1.2	0.1	2.5	0.0	1.8
Robbery	3.3	1.9	1.9	2.0	0.3	1.8	0.1	1.6
Other violent	14.4	2.3	8.1	2.7	1.2	1.7	0.9	1.9
Property	21.8	6.2	10.3	6.3	3.1	2.9	1.2	2.9
Burglary	10.8	3.8	5.7	3.5	0.9	2.1	0.4	2.0
SMV	8.4	2.7	3.6	2.5	0.7	1.8	0.2	1.4
Stealing	15.4	3.0	8.0	3.2	1.8	2.0	0.8	2.0
Other property	9.6	2.6	4.7	2.3	1.2	2.2	0.4	2.2
Drug	8.3	1.7	4.2	1.8	1.4	1.6	1.1	1.6
Drink	5.7	1.2	1.9	1.1	2.4	1.1	1.2	1.1
Traffic	12.2	3.7	6.5	3.7	2.6	2.2	1.6	2.1

Table 11 (cont.)

	Indigenous				Non-Indigenous			
	1984		1994		1984		1994	
	Prevalence by age 21 (%)	Rate per active offender	Prevalence by age 21 (%)	Rate per active offender	Prevalence by age 21 (%)	Rate per active offender	Prevalence by age 21 (%)	Rate per active offender
Disorder	21.0	3.9	10.7	4.6	2.6	2.0	1.4	2.4
Breach	7.7	2.6	7.2	5.5	0.4	1.9	0.7	3.5
Other	9.7	1.7	5.7	2.2	0.8	1.4	0.5	1.5
All	32.2	12.0	14.3	16.7	8.6	3.7	4.3	4.5
All (excl. breaches)	32.2	11.4	14.3	14.0	8.6	3.6	4.3	4.0

Source: Payne et al. (2016) – *Trajectories of two NSW Birth Cohorts [Computer File]*

With regard to changes in onset and chronicity, there are a number of important preexisting differences that complicate the comparative analysis. For example, early onset offending was relatively rare among the Indigenous population, comprising just 1.1 percent of all Indigenous people born in 1984, but was more prevalent by a factor of 10 when compared to non-Indigenous young people born in the same year (0.1%). By 1994, the population prevalence of early onset offending increased among Indigenous offenders (from 1.1 to 1.2%), but has remained relatively constant within the non-Indigenous cohort (0.1% in both the 1984 and 1994 cohorts).

Adolescent-onset offending is also disproportionally more prevalent among Indigenous youth (Table 12). In the 1984 birth cohort, 11 percent of young Indigenous people had contact with the criminal justice system for the first time between the ages of thirteen and seventeen years. This compared to 3.4 percent of the non-Indigenous youth in the same year. By 1994, the population prevalence of adolescent-onset offending among Indigenous youth fell to 5 percent, while the prevalence among non-Indigenous youth fell to 1.7 percent. In both cases, the prevalence of adolescent-onset offending declined, although the decline was greater among the Indigenous population.

An important and notable fact in these data is that the vast majority of Indigenous youth first have contact with the criminal justice system as children or adolescents. That is, adult onset offending, at least until age twenty-one in our data, is comparatively rare (4.6% in the 1984 cohort). The opposite is true for the non-Indigenous birth cohorts where it appears more likely that non-Indigenous young people will first have contact with the criminal justice system as young adults (5% in 1984). In both cases, the population prevalence of adult onset offending declined between 1984 and 1994, although it is worth highlighting that decline was considerably greater among Indigenous youth (down by 72%) than non-Indigenous youth (down by 48%).

Finally, taking a broader view of these onset data we note that within the offending populations of both groups, the distribution of offenders by onset age was relatively unchanged for non-Indigenous young people between 1984 and 1994. The crime-drop, it seems, has been associated with a broadly proportionate decrease in prevalence across all categories of onset. For Indigenous youth, however, the story is different. Between 1984 and 1994, there was a disproportionate decline in the prevalence of adult onset offending and no decline in the prevalence of early onset offending.

The data on chronicity also point to some notable differences between Indigenous and non-Indigenous young people in NSW, although again, these differences are difficult to interpret given the distributional differences between both groups. The majority of young Indigenous people are arrested and

Table 12 Onset and chronicity, by Indigenous status (1984 and 1994)

| | Indigenous | | | | Non-indigenous | | | |
| | 1984 | | 1994 | | 1984 | | 1994 | |
	% of offenders	% of population	% of offenders	% of population	% of offenders	% of population	% of offenders	% of population
Age of onset								
Early (10–12 years)	6.8	1.1	16.4	1.2	0.9	0.1	1.8	0.1
Adolescent (13–17 years)	65.9	11.1	69.8	5.0	40.1	3.4	38.7	1.7
Adult (18–20 years)	27.3	4.6	13.8	1.0	59.1	5.0	59.5	2.6
Chronicity								
Once-only	13.0	2.2	8.0	0.6	43.6	3.7	39.5	1.7
2–4 offenses	26.9	4.5	19.3	1.4	36.6	3.1	34.3	1.5
5+ offenses	60.2	10.1	72.7	5.2	19.8	1.7	26.3	1.1

Source: Payne et al. (2016) – *Trajectories of two NSW Birth Cohorts [Computer File]*

convicted for five or more offenses. This category of chronic offending comprised 60 percent of the Indigenous birth cohort in 1984 and 73 percent of the 1994 cohort. Once-only offending is comparatively rare among Indigenous young people, representing just 13 percent of the 1984 cohort and 8 percent of the 1994 cohort. For non-Indigenous offenders, the reverse is true with once-only offending being more prevalent than either moderate or chronic offending.

Between 1984 and 1994, the population prevalence of once-only offending among Indigenous youth declined by 72 percent (from 2.2% to 0.6%). Moderate offending also declined by 67 percent, while chronic offending declined by a little less than 50 percent (from 10% to 5.1%). This disproportionate change is the reason why chronic offenders now represent the largest group of Indigenous offenders born in 1994 (71%).[12] For non-Indigenous youth, the decline in both once-only and moderate offending was approximately 50 percent, while the decline in chronic offending was just 32 percent. Whereas the overall decline in prevalence seemed relatively consistent between Indigenous and non-Indigenous young people, it seems that the within-group changes were anything but consistent.

Perhaps the most important takeaway message from these data is in the relative overrepresentation of young Indigenous people in the criminal justice system. On the positive side, the overrepresentation of young Indigenous people seems to have narrowed in the context of the NSW crime-drop such that, proportional to population, there seems to have been a larger reduction in the prevalence of criminal justice contact for young Indigenous people. In 1984, for example, the Indigenous-born population was 3.7 times as likely to have had contact with the criminal justice system by twenty-one years of age. This decreased to an overrepresentation rate of 3.3 for the 1994 cohort. Less positively, the average offense rate of both Indigenous and non-Indigenous offenders increased between 1984 and 1994, although, this increase was greater for young Indigenous offenders. Consequently, Indigenous young people in the 1994 cohort were responsible for a larger share of their cohort's overall crime count, increasing from 33 percent in 1984, to 40 percent in 1994.

10 Conclusion

Using a comparative analysis of two Australian birth cohorts, this study has sought to contribute new evidence to the global search for causes, correlates, and consequences of the international crime-drop. Our analyses, framed

---

[12] This, of course, raises the more general issue as to why this pattern emerges. Is it because of differential offending by Indigenous youth with respect to the kinds of crimes that draw the attention of justice officials, differential enforcement against these individuals by the justice system, or some combination of both (see Piquero, 2008).

through the lens of developmental and life-course criminology, contribute to a landscape of empirical research that has demonstrated a significant and sustained decline in crime, predominantly youth crime, in almost all high-income (developed economy) countries throughout the Americas, Europe, and in the Asia-Pacific region. While the decline has not been universal in either degree or kind, and while there is some very-recent indications of a reversal of trend in (and/or within) some countries, the near-concurrent and widespread experience of this youth-based phenomenon demands that we look beyond the very-local and parochial explanations offered to date and, instead, search for complementary mechanisms that are more generalizable. The theoretical and empirical frameworks of developmental and life-course criminology offer such an opportunity.

Australia – the location of this study – has been no exception in its experience of the crime-drop. Since the turn of the century, all categories of crime have been in decline and, like elsewhere in the world, these decreases have been most pronounced amongst young people. What distinguishes Australia is the relatively late timing of the decline (in most other countries the decline started in the late 1980s or early 1990s), and the precedence of property offending as the first category of crime to trend downward. In fact, an oft-forgotten feature in the rush to globalize the crime-drop story is the often very unique experience, both in timing and in kind, at the local level, and this variation ought to feature more prominently in future cross-cultural and comparative analyses of this phenomenon. For the present study, we take advantage of the somewhat delayed timing of the Australian crime-drop to select two birth cohorts of NSW children and explore their criminal justice contact using one of Australia's most comprehensive longitudinal criminal justice databases. Although born only ten years apart, our cohorts were adolescents in two very different periods. The first were born in 1984 and were adolescents before the crime-drop. The second were born in 1994 and were adolescents after the crime-drop had commenced. The data we used has full coverage of their criminal justice contact between the ages of ten and twenty-one years and we exploit this opportunity to compare their criminal career parameters.

Overview of Key Findings

Of the results presented in this study, we make five key observations. First, members of the 1994 birth cohort were responsible for approximately 10,000 fewer offenses than their peers born in 1984. This equated to a 39 percent fall in the total quantum of offenses committed to the equivalent age of twenty-one. This decline, in just ten years, is consistent with the wider push to recognize the crime-drop as a predominantly youth-based phenomenon and reaffirms the need to consider adolescent-relevant causes for the crime-drop. Within this, we noted that the reduction was greatest for property and other acquisitive offenses, although every offense type bar one (breach and justice-related offenses) was lower in volume for the 1994 cohort. The disproportionate decline in the total volume of property offending suggests that either this type of offending has become harder to commit or less attractive to would-be offenders.

Second, the drop in crime was disproportionally driven by a decline in the prevalence of criminal participation, and less so by a decline in the frequency of offending among active offenders. For this Australian data, the population prevalence of offending by age twenty-one fell by almost 50 percent (from 9.5% among the 1984 cohort to 4.8% among the 1994 cohort). In real terms, this means that there were 3,555 fewer offenders in the criminal justice system by age twenty-one. Even if these offenders only committed one offense, their absence from the criminal justice system would account for one-third of the 10,000 crimes that were saved between the 1984 and 1994 cohorts. Later analysis confirms that the decline between these two cohorts was overwhelmingly driven by the disappearance of once-only or low-frequency offenders, rather than any substantial fall in the size or offending patterns of chronic offenders.

Third, for those who did have contact with the criminal justice system, there was almost no difference in the average age of onset. This means that while active offending might have been prevented for some, or reduced for others, it was not delayed for those who did embark on a criminal career. This is an important finding because it suggests that whatever caused the crime-drop might not have been universal or experienced by everyone. It is notable, for example, that the population prevalence of very-early onset offending did not change. Instead, the first age-graded differences between the two cohorts do not emerge until thirteen or fourteen years of age.

Fourth, the frequency of offending among active offenders (lambda) increased in the 1994 cohort. This is not a surprising result given the substantial disappearance of once-only or low-rate offenders. In fact, these data show that while active offending rates increased, this story is somewhat complicated because the upward trend was largely the result of a distributional shift caused by the dropout of infrequent offenders. The actual rate of offending among chronic offenders (those who committed five or more offenses) did not change between the cohorts and this, once again suggests that whatever caused the crime decline did not equally affect or benefit those who would go on to become chronic offenders.

Finally, the findings were generally the same for both men and women, and were only slightly more favorable (at least in terms of the overall change in prevalence) for Indigenous young people. Coupled with the disparities above, these results suggest that while the drivers of the crime decline might not have equally benefited the early onset and chronic-offender populations, they have been generally equal in their impact on once-only or low-rate offenders of different demographic characteristics. There is a sense here that the cause of the crime-drop has been general, but disproportionate in its beneficial effects for those who are likely to have early and frequent contact with the criminal justice system.

Developmental and Life-Course Explanations

These empirical findings provide a unique perspective on the potential causes and correlates of the crime decline, but theory is still needed to bridge the divide between what has occurred and why. What remains is the need to explain why a large proportion of once-only or low-rate offenders have avoided formal contact with the criminal justice system, while the cohort of early onset and chronic offenders have neither disappeared nor lessened their offending to any great extent. As was highlighted earlier, we believe that contemporary developmental and life-course criminological theory offers some insight and a new lens through which future analyses of these and other data can be framed.

The decline in prevalence, we do not believe, is the consequence of some dramatic shift to the underlying distribution of the propensity to offend. Specifically, it is unlikely in our view that such dramatic changes could have occurred in this relatively short period of just ten years. For example, in their *General Theory of Crime*, Gottfredson and Hirschi (1990) argue in favor of low self-control as the general cause of crime, which, in their view, manifests as antisocial and criminal behavior when the opportunities to do so are present and prevalent. Accordingly, Gottfredson and Hirschi described a propensity-event framework where population-level crime rates are the consequence of stable between-individual differences in propensity (self-control) and age-varying opportunities that make possible the commission of criminal activities. Under this framework, for there to be a substantial decline in crime between two birth cohorts, there would need to have been a large aggregate improvement in population-level self-control, or some fundamental change to the opportunities and events that make crime possible. From our perspective, and consistent with Gottfredson and Hirschi's own view about historical variations in the age-crime curve, large dramatic improvements in the population distribution of self-control would be unlikely.[13]

---

[13] We recognize of course that testing self-control at the aggregate level is not what the theorists originally had in mind, but there has been some movement in this direction (see Diamond et al., 2018; Eisner, 2014).

We recall from their earlier contributions that low self-control is the consequence of poor parenting and failed socialization in childhood. Large shifts in the distribution of this general cause would need to have been preceded by some dramatic improvement in the quality of parenting or the efficacy of childhood pro-socialization. From our perspective, it is difficult to imagine this occurring in just ten years, especially to the degree suggested in these data and in the absence of any other Australian sources confirming parallel changes of this magnitude.

Assuming that persistent population heterogeneity continues to define a stable distribution of low self-control (or other propensities to offend), then the crime-drop is more likely to have been a consequence of a change in the opportunity structures that once made crime possible and more prevalent. For Gottfredson and Hirschi, opportunity is the key to understanding when a crime occurs even if low self-control is the ultimate cause. Without the opportunity to offend, propensity may not be realized, muted, or redirected, and it is for this reason that we believe there is a need to further explore the opportunity structures that govern youthful antisocial behavior. This will ultimately involve questioning whether these structures have limited criminal opportunities for contemporary cohorts of young people and redirected those with moderate-to-low self-control into other non-criminal activities. We also note that crime, according to Gottfredson and Hirschi, is the manifestation of low self-control because it is a fun, short-term, impulsive act that satisfies immediate interests and needs over longer-term consequences. Through this lens, the crime-drop is likely to have resulted either because the opportunities to offend have diminished in prevalence, or because other non-criminal activities have emerged as sufficiently analogous to crime – activities that are fun, risky, individually rewarding, and sufficient to meet the short-term impulsive needs of those with relatively low self-control.

Opportunity structures also feature heavily in Farrington's (2003) Integrated Cognitive and Antisocial Potential (ICAP) theory in which he delineates long- and short-term antisocial potential as cocontributors to the advent of crime. Long-term AP develops as a consequence of accumulated developmental disadvantage and is linked to crime largely through the structuring of opportunities for crime over the life-course. It is broadly analogous to Gottfredson and Hirschi's depiction of low self-control as the principle cause of crime across the life-course. Short-term AP reflects the more immediate energizing factors that promote crime in the moment. For Farrington, crime is most likely to occur frequently and persistently when both short- and long-term AP are high for a young person. The vast majority of youth, however, have low long-term AP, and so their brief involvement in crime, usually in adolescence, is the consequence of the powerful effects of those short-term AP energizing factors such as boredom, frustration, the desire for material gain, the desire to maintain status among peers, and the need for excitement or sexual gratification. Through this lens, the crime-drop may be similarly explained through the changing nature of youthful opportunities that have either limited the power/potency of AP energizing factors, or redressed these needs in other legitimate ways. The move to digital communication and digital socialization, for example, may have reduced boredom and frustration as more and more young people find pleasure and independence in digital contexts. Peer structures, and the relative importance of peer status, may have lessened in value as more young people navigate multiple peer and social groups both on and offline. Also, the now free and immediate availability of pornography online, as well as the opportunities for risk taking and thrill seeking in digital and virtual spaces, may have de-energized those traditional forms of AP described by ICAP (Farrington, 2003).

Although both the *General Theory of Crime* and ICAP point to the importance of changing opportunity structures, it remains unclear why these changes seem not to have affected the prevalence of early onset offending, nor resulted in a lower rate of offending among chronic offenders. The presupposition of static theories is that all potential offenders are affected equally by the same causal process and only the quantity and frequency of offending should vary relative to the degree of latent propensity. In principle, therefore, what has prevented low-rate offenders from having any contact with the criminal justice system should have exerted at least some preventative pressure on all offenders and thus produced fewer early onset offenders (or delayed their offending) and resulted in lower average offending rates across all categories. Clearly, this did not happen. In fact, what these data suggest is that those most vulnerable young people in the 1994 cohort did not benefit from whatever caused crime to decline.

There are several possible reasons for this. First, vulnerable youth may not have experienced, to the same degree as their peers, a change in opportunity structures. This, we believe, is plausible because vulnerable youth are also among the most socially and economically disadvantaged (Moffitt, 1993). If the transition to a digital and online social economy is at least part of the crime-drop story, then it is unlikely that our most vulnerable youth will have been its greatest beneficiaries. Second, perhaps the disappearance of key short-term energizing factors and opportunities only affect those young people with low levels of long-term potential. In other words, perhaps the relative effect of these changing opportunity structures differs depending on the degree to which a young person has already accumulated long-term criminal potential. Crime may only become less attractive, less essential, and less fun for those youth who have low or no long-term criminal potential. For the small minority likely to start early and offend often, these changes may have little bearing in the presence of strong latent potential. Third, maybe the causes of crime are not general at all, but rather, the causes may in fact be qualitatively different for early onset offenders and these causes have not fundamentally changed in the last two decades.

Here we see value in Moffitt's (1993) dual taxonomy that explicitly argues for differential causal explanations in developmental criminology. For example, in our data, it appears that the crime-drop has been driven by a substantial change in the prevalence of adolescent-onset offenders: a specific group theorized by Moffitt (1993) as not, in the main, developmentally, intellectually, or psychologically disadvantaged. Rather, such offenders have typically had a "normal" upbringing, in relatively stable homes and with limited adverse interactions with their parents and other figures of authority. They are, in many respects, the "normative" group of young people whose antisocial behavior is not the result of any underlying predisposition, but rather the result of risk seeking and mimicking behaviors borne from status and maturational conflicts. Their criminal participation is largely incidental, opportunistic, and short lived, unless formal criminal processing forecloses prosocial opportunities and ensnares these young adolescents into a pattern of structural and accumulated disadvantage that later promotes persistent criminal participation. This type of adolescent-limited offender is distinguished from their chronic peers because they do not have the psychological and cognitive deficits, nor the failed parent-child relationships that characterize early onset and life-course persistent offending.

For Moffitt, the large and disproportionate fall in the prevalence of adolescent-limited offending might be rooted in social changes that have structured new opportunities for the typical young person to traverse the challenges of adolescence without the same risks of formal criminal justice contact. Perhaps, incidental offending has become more difficult and more risky with increased securitization and target hardening, particularly for the less serious acquisitive offenses that have traditionally marked the start of adolescent onset offending. This heightened risk may factor increasingly into the would-be adolescent offender's decision-making and this, in turn, may have affected a decline in the overall criminal participation of adolescent-limited offending. Farrington (2003) similarly argued that cognitive processes were an important determinant for the translation of AP into criminal behavior, and risk is seen as a key component of the decision-making process. Another possible explanation might be found in the changing nature of non-criminal adolescent opportunities and the diminishing influence of maturational status as a motivation for antisocial behavior. Alcohol, tobacco, and other drug-use rates are lower now than at any other time in Australian history (Australian Institute of Health and Welfare 2017). Pornography is now much more accessible via the Internet. The historical objects and status symbols of adulthood, typically access to sexualized activities and material gains, are now more widespread and much more accessible to young people. If, as Moffitt contends, a large proportion of adolescent-limited offending exists because young people covet (and act in antisocial ways to attain) adulthood status, then it is possible that the large fall in the prevalence of adolescent-limited offending has occurred at a time when the symbols of maturation and adulthood status have disappeared or weakened in the contemporary context (and perhaps shifted online).

Alternatively, there is an emerging body of literature that talks about the phenomenon of "emerging adulthood" as a new interim step between adolescence and adulthood (Arnett, 2000). In this literature, emerging adulthood defines a period of increasing social autonomy without a full transition to financial independence. These older adolescents are typically unmarried and living at home with their parents, but socially independent and autonomous. Arnett called this a period of the "roleless role" because emerging adults can participate in a wide variety of activities, but are not then constrained by any of "role requirements" that are demanded of *real* adults (Arnett 2000). Perhaps "adulthood" is no longer coveted by the adolescent-limited offender and the "acting out" in frustration becomes less common as the transition to adulthood becomes more gradual and the goal of true adulthood less desirable when most of the benefits can be realized earlier in the life course.

Finally, for Moffitt, mimicry is also an important element of adolescent-limited offending because, in their pursuit of the symbols and freedoms of adulthood, young adolescents are attracted to the apparent freedom and early maturational success of their more chronic and early onset peers. They are attracted to antisocial behavior of those with stronger antisocial dispositions because it appears these young peers, through their antisocial behavior, have succeeded in bridging the maturational gap. Mimicry of this kind may be less attractive nowadays, in part because the symbols of adulthood status have changed, and partly because the low-level offenses have become more risky. In addition, it is possible that the structuring of social opportunities has changed such that regular and ongoing contact with chronic offending youth has diminished. Consider the now well-documented increase in social digital connectivity among today's youth and the increasing prevalence of "digital-play" as a replacement for physical play in and after school.

We contrast this with the finding that there was no decline in the population prevalence of early onset offending – a population that has long been shown to be relatively rare in any population cohort (Piquero et al., 2003). Rare as they might be, it is striking that the relative prevalence of this group did not decline by 1994 and that their longer-term trajectories were, in fact, less favorable than their 1984 peers. For Moffitt (1993) and other developmental and life-course criminologists, early onset offending is a particularly important marker for the development of persistent longer-term criminal trajectories. Moffitt specifically described this group as "life course persistent" (LCP) since their proclivity to antisocial behavior starts early and lasts longer than any other group of offenders. For Moffitt, LCP offending is the consequence of psychological and cognitive deficits that first manifest as fractious parent–child relationships and, later, as weak prosocial attachments (Moffitt, 2003). Crime for the young LCP offender is partly a consequence of limited cognitive and decision-making capacity and partly a consequence of the accumulated consequences of their early life disadvantage. Although Farrington (2003) does not define a specialized or particular group of offenders, he too argues that early onset offending is a hallmark criminal career experience of those young kids who develop long-term antisocial potential from an early age.

That over the course of the Australia crime-drop there has been no change in the population prevalence of early onset offending suggests that whatever has driven the decline in crime did not ameliorate the power of those factors that caused the offending of this small but core segment of the population. We have, perhaps, not achieved much in terms of improving the outcomes of those psychosocial or cognitively disadvantaged youth, nor have we achieved much in terms of reducing or minimizing their long-term contact with the criminal justice system. Further, their persistence in both prevalence and long-term offending suggests that they have either not experienced or not benefited from the social changes underlying the crime-drop, or they have resisted those changes. In our view, early onset offending is the result of some accumulated disadvantage that sets the foreground for the antisocial behavior at home and in school. We might imagine, as Moffitt (1993) and Farrington (2003) argue, that this disadvantage is, in large part, the consequence of psychosocial or cognitive deficits that occur naturally (and at roughly the same rate) in all cohorts of the population. These youth have a proclivity to antisocial behavior that remains objectionable within many social contexts, and that is responded to in a manner that increases the longer-term propensity to crime. So strong is the accumulated disadvantage of this unfavorable childhood environment that broad social changes, of the likes described earlier, are of little effect in redirecting the early onset offender away from eventual involvement in the criminal justice system. Securitization and target hardening of low-level property offenses, for example, may well discourage adolescent-limited or early adult offenders, but is not likely enough to counter the strong underlying antisocial potential of the early onset offender. Further, the restructuring of peer group and other social opportunities into the online and digital domains may have relatively little impact on early onset youth whose antisocial potential continues to manifest as sanctionable behavior in school and at home, and whose proclivity to short-term and impulsive acts cannot be easily sated in the online world.

Finally, and perhaps the greatest insight provided by these comparative data is the support they lend to developmental and life-course criminology's most fundamental tenant – that the correlates of crime, and of the individual criminal career parameters, can vary at different stages of the life-course (Blumstein et al., 1986). Set against the backdrop of a seemingly universal cause that has affected both young boys, girls, and Indigenous Australians, there is still a stark inequality between early onset and adolescent onset offenders. This leads us to believe that the cause of crime-drop did not benefit early onset offenders, most likely because their onset and persistence in crime is probably driven by different causal mechanisms. From our perspective, the crime-drop is a near-natural experiment that has lent its support to the kinds of multicausal frameworks proposed by Farrington (2003) or typological frameworks proposed by Moffitt (1993).

Limitations

Before considering the implications of this study, we pause for a moment to reflect on what is missing in these data and what consequences this has for our conclusions. First, our data are censored at age twenty-one. We do not know how the criminal trajectories of these two cohorts would unfold throughout their twenties (and beyond) and whether the cohorts will converge again in later life. Sampson and Laub (2003) remind us that criminal trajectories are most certainly not fixed and that there remains a great deal of heterogeneity in later-life outcomes, not all of which is predictable from early developmental experiences. One particular point of interest will be in the comparative advent and prevalence of late-onset offending (Gomez-Smith & Piquero, 2005; Zara & Farrington, 2009) and whether those 1994-born adolescents who avoided criminal justice contact emerge in greater numbers as new entrants to the criminal justice system as adults. Krohn et al. (2013), for example, theorize adult-onset offending as the emergence of antisocial adults who as adolescents were "cocooned" by their affluent parents and wider prosocial environment. These adolescents, they argue, have moderate to high propensity for antisocial behavior, but avoided formal contact with the criminal justice system because their family and social environments protected them from its adverse consequences. Although in this study we cannot measure the emergence of adult-onset offending to its fullest extent, we might imagine its prevalence will be higher in the 1994 cohort as this cohort transitions into adulthood and departs from the situational and opportunistic mechanisms that we believe have helped to mute adolescent-limited criminal participation.

We are also mindful that this study relies on officially recorded administrative data as the foundation of its comparative analysis. This raises important questions about the potential administrative, procedural, and data-recording changes that might have affected an artificial decline in crime and this requires careful consideration. In our view, the sheer magnitude of the differences between these two birth cohorts is not likely to be the result of any significant or dramatic change in police data recording or reporting practices. Such a significant shift would not likely occur in just ten years, at least not without being formally announced by the NSW Police or identified by those charged with independent reporting on NSW police statistics. We also believe that such system-wide changes would manifest as a muting effect on all offenders, including the trajectories of early onset offenders. This was not the case. Of course, this is not to say that some small incremental changes in administrative practices have not contributed, in part, to our results. There is evidence, after all, that some directed and focused police practices are effective in disrupting crime at places and, in turn, by those engaging in criminal activity (e.g., Telep & Weisburd, 2012). Rather, we believe that the results and substantive conclusions presented here at are not likely to be the spurious outcome of some wider transformation in police or court-level administrative procedures.

Conclusions and Implications

For as long as police statistics have been systematically recorded, the crime-drop of the 1990s has been the greatest ever observed in both magnitude and length. The extant empirical literature points to a largely international phenomenon, one that has manifested at the local level with great heterogeneity in both nature and timing but that has shared one consistent theme – that the crime-drop phenomenon has been predominantly the consequence of dramatic shifts in the criminal justice system contact of young people. Australia, where the present study is set, has been no exception – having a geographically heterogeneous experience of the crime-drop throughout the 2000s that has been driven, in all states and territories, by a disproportionate fall in the incidence of youth crime. Both here and around the world, the complexity of this international story has left criminological scholars wondering whether the crime-drop is just an incidental and almost accidental phenomenon, or whether the root causes can be found in the more purposeful and directed efforts of programs and policies that have emerged from contemporary criminological theory.

Focusing on the criminal justice system contact of young people from two Australian birth cohorts born ten years apart in 1984 and 1994, respectively, this study provides new insights. We compare their criminal trajectories from age ten to twenty-one with the view to identifying who in the population was most likely to have contributed to the crime-drop and what this tells us about its potential origins. Recognizing the decline as a youth phenomenon, our approach was guided through a life-course lens as we searched potential developmental explanations. In the younger of the two cohorts (those who entered adolescence only after the crime-drop had begun), we expected to find the greatest reductions in offending among those who were the traditionally early onset and on the path to chronic and persistent offending. After all, ever since the first of the Philadelphia Birth Cohort studies (Wolfgang et al., 1972) criminology has asserted that the greatest and most efficient crime-preventative potential rests in those interventions that target the disproportionately small number of offenders who commit the greatest share of crime.[14] What we found, instead, was that the most likely contributor to the great Australian crime-drop was the substantial absence of the once-high number of incidental or very low rate offenders. But for a few small shifts, the population prevalence of early onset offending and the subsequent adolescent offending trajectories of these at-risk youth were remarkably consistent with their peers born ten years earlier.

For criminology, these results demand deep reflection and introspection. They bring new light to some of our greatest theoretical debates and, in so doing, may represent a turning point in how we think about the policy and programmatic intersections of criminal careers and crime prevention.[15] For example, as a scholarly community, we remain divided about whether our discipline should prioritize the study of criminality or the criminal potential of places and spaces. We have been divided on the question of whether rule breaking and antisocial behavior are inherently unnatural to the human and social condition, or whether such behavior is ubiquitous and normative in the absence of internal and external controls. We have been required to adjudicate the relative merits of individual-level intensive intervention versus situational crime prevention. These debates have inspired a generation of scholars who, despite their differences, all seek to achieve the same end – a lower rate of crime

---

[14] A parallel also exists with respect to the community of place, where it has long been argued that since a small number of addresses are responsible for a great proportion of calls for service and crimes, or hot spots, then police should target their resources on this similar "chronic few" locations (see e.g., Sherman et al., 1989; Weisburd, 2018).

[15] In his Presidential Address to the American Society of Criminology in 2003, Laub (2004) discussed specific turning points in criminological theory and research that launched the field in new and different directions.

and fewer victims in the community. Our results do not resolve these debates. They do, however, suggest that the largest and most protracted crime-drop ever experienced in Australia was not likely the product of interventions aimed at reducing the volume of offending among high-risk offenders. Rather, it was most likely wider social changes that restructured criminal opportunities and made crime less likely and less rewarding to the wider population of incidental offenders. This is not to say that intensive and individual-oriented early or developmental interventions are not an essential piece to the crime prevention puzzle, only that a comprehensive strategy should not ignore the potential power of time, place, and opportunity-based interventions for the much larger low-risk offender community.

Beyond this, as the first longitudinal dual-cohort analysis of the crime-drop, our results raise a number of other important questions for policy and practice. First, the large and disproportionate decline in the population prevalence of infrequent and temporary adolescent-onset offenders is a welcome result, driving the volume of crime down by 40 percent and significantly lessening the processing and procedural impost on police, the courts, and the institutions of corrective service. In our view, since juvenile and criminal justice contact has been found to be criminogenic for some offenders (Bhati & Piquero, 2008; Gatti et al., 2009) and since adolescent-onset offending has the potential to become chronic if prosocial opportunities are foreclosed or if persons become ensnared (Moffitt, 1993), this relative saving to the criminal justice system will be even greater as the 1994 cohort gets older. This will come as welcome news for those managing resources in the juvenile and criminal justice systems, although it equally raises important and difficult questions about the need to redistribute resources within the criminal justice system or from the criminal justice system to other social services.

What happens once this 1994 cohort enters their mid-to-late twenties is anyone's guess, however, we predict that a number of them will enter the criminal justice system as adults. The relative prevalence of adult-onset offending will likely increase as these "cocooned" (Krohn et al., 2013) adolescents transition through emerging adulthood and take on greater adult responsibilities without the protection of their parents and family. If we are correct, then some of the criminal justice savings of the crime-drop may need to be refocused into prevention and early intervention strategies that target emerging adults and their specific criminogenic needs. Historically, adult-onset offending has been somewhat of an afterthought for criminal career analysis – an artifact that was largely inconsistent with the core thesis of stability and change. Going forward, we may need to revisit the centrality of the adult-onset phenomenon and grow our investment in research and interventions that are suitably targeted to this kind of delayed offending.

Of course, these predictions need to be weighed against the relative stagnation of early onset and chronic offending because, while it is true that there is less crime and fewer offenders, those who remain in the criminal justice system look relatively more serious and are responsible for a larger share of the crime count and exert significant financial costs on society (Cohen & Piquero, 2009). To be clear, this is not because they are necessarily more serious than earlier generations of youth, at least not significantly, but because they are becoming an increasingly concentrated group of clients in the criminal justice system: what Canela-Cacho and his colleagues (1997) referred to as "stochastic selectivity." In Australia, there is a popular misconception that young people are becoming more serious and committing more crime and this is a view that is held even by criminal justice practitioners and members of the judiciary (see Bishop 2006). It may seem difficult to reconcile this against the empirical evidence of the crime-drop, however it is our view that these perceptions are not incongruous with the empirical evidence in that they reflect an increasingly concentrated chronic-offender population with whom criminal justice practitioners have relatively greater and more regular contact. Ensuring that this misperception of a "youth crime crisis" does not translate into an unnecessarily punitive approach will be an important outcome of these data.

Second, though difficult to test, there are some positive indications that investment in early intervention and diversion efforts have contributed to the crime-drop. The lower rates of early offending among early onset offenders is a positive sign that in the earliest days of contact there might have been active efforts to limit the extent of formal processing. It is difficult to know how much of the decline in adolescent and early adult offending was also the consequence of early intervention and diversion, although we do not discount the possibility. Our concern, however, lies in the possible individual-level net-widening effect that might result after diversion has been formally introduced and rolled out across the criminal justice system. In our data, we see a persistent difference between the 1984 and 1994 early onset offenders, with the latter having higher average rates of offending after their fourteenth birthday. We are concerned that this difference might signal a move to higher rates of detection and a more punitive response to chronic offending once the young offender is seen to have exhausted his or her diversionary options. Put simply, the increase in diversionary practice for all offenders may also increase the spotlight on chronic offending and reframe this behavior as a rejection of the concessions already made through earlier efforts at diversion. There is a risk that diversion, although beneficial to the majority of would-be adolescent-limited offenders, has the potential to increase the surveillance and detection of those who fail to adhere to their diversion conditions. The considerable spike in "breach" offending, particularly as an onset offense, lends support to this concern.

Third, there is little these data can provide in terms of understanding the potential for displacement. The assumption of our analysis is that the overwhelming majority of young adolescent offenders simply stopped engaging in crime, but there is real potential that some of this antisocial behavior has been displaced into places or contexts that have limited opportunities for detection. Perhaps the most likely case is that some antisocial behavior has been displaced into the digital world, such as online bullying, the participation in dark-web markets, and identity theft–related offenses. What we know is that recorded crime has dropped significantly as a consequence of a substantial fall in criminal participation. What remains to be learned is whether some of these young people have found other ways to engage in antisocial behavior that is equally or potentially more harmful. Only self-report studies will help to reveal this potential displacement and evidence of its increase will be important for furthering a developmental and life-course criminological view of the international crime-drop.

Fourth, while our focus in the current study was on understanding the crime-drop between two cohorts with involvement in the justice system, there is a growing recognition, aided by research focused on the decision-making patterns of adolescents, that juvenile offenders are "more impulsive, short-sighted, and responsive to immediate rewards and less likely to consider long-term consequences" (Monahan et al., 2015, p. 577). As a result, the justice system responses to adolescent offending should take these features into account and respond in a developmentally appropriate manner. In the United States, the Supreme Court has held that certain severe punishments are no longer permissible for juvenile offenders and some states are considering extending their juvenile court jurisdictions beyond age eighteen. In Australia, there are ongoing calls to increase the age of criminal responsibility from ten years to fourteen years. When this is coupled with the significant movements in Europe to provide developmentally appropriate responses to offenders between ages eighteen and twenty-five (Matthews et al., 2018), it is clear that there are strong views that support continued efforts at providing rehabilitative services to adolescent offenders (Piquero et al., 2010) and even more support in favor of financially supporting early childhood prevention in lieu of more (and longer) punishments (Nagin et al., 2006). There are many evidence-based strategies in this regard, including early family/parent training programs (Piquero et al., 2009, 2016), where it has been shown that early investments made in childhood will have positive reverberations over the life-course. Scaling up such efforts is

a worthwhile goal and it will be good to see the extent to which these investments alter the criminal offending patterns of subsequent cohorts of juvenile
offenders in the future.

Finally, we return to where we started and remind ourselves of the first
Philadelphia Birth Cohort study (Wolfgang et al., 1972) and its call for selectivity in criminal justice policy. Since then, the orientation of consequent
policies and programs has been largely geared toward a focus on individual-
level preventative actions that target the small population of offenders who are
responsible for the highest volume of crime. Our study may offer, as Laub
noted, a turning point away from this single way of thinking. Herein, we
observed that the single greatest and most protracted decline in crime in
Australia's history was not the consequence of criminal justice programs
targeting chronic offenders – though many of these exists – but the change in
offending among those least likely to offend. To the best of our knowledge, this
has occurred without any deliberate intent by government and without any
specifically dedicated programs or interventions by police, courts, or correc-
tions. Put simply, significant quantities of crime can be prevented, it seems, by
affecting the decisions and choices of the majority whose crime is most likely
infrequent, opportunistic, and incidental. How to achieve and sustain this
requires much more research, but, if done well, it need not be at significant
cost. This is especially important now that in some places, including in
Australia, the almost two decades of crime decline is showing some early
signs of reversal. NSW, for example, has recently recorded an 8.8 percent
increase in retail theft for the September quarter of 2019 (NSW Bureau of
Crime Statistics and Research, 2019) while to the south, the Victorian Crime
Statistics Agency (CSA) has also recently reported an increase of 1.6 percent in
the overall crime rate for that state (CSA, 2019). Understanding those mechanisms that caused such a large number of young people to avoid crime may help
to sustain the crime-drop for years to come.

References

Aebi, M. F., & Linde, A. (2010). Is there a crime drop in Western Europe? *European Journal on Criminal Policy and Research, 16*(4), 251–277.

Aebi, M. F., & Linde, A. (2012). Conviction statistics as an indicator of crime trends in Europe from 1990 to 2006. *European Journal on Criminal Policy and Research, 18*(1), 1303–1144. doi:http://dx.doi.org/10.1007/s10610-011-9166-7

Agnew, R. (1992). Foundation for a general strain theory of crime and delinquency. *Criminology, 30*(1), 47–88.

Agnew, R. (1997). Stability and change in crime over the life course: A strain theory explanation. In T. P. Thornberry (ed.), *Developmental Theories of Crime and Delinquency* (Vol. 7, pp. 101–132). New Jersey: Transaction Publishers.

Andersen, L. H., Anker, A. S. T., & Andersen, S. H. (2016). A formal decomposition of declining youth crime in Denmark. *Demographic Research, 35*, 1303–1316.

Arnett, J. J. (2000). Emerging adulthood: A theory of development from the late teens through the twenties. *American Psychologist, 55*(5), 469–480. doi:10.1037//0003-066x.55.5.469

Australian Bureau of Statistics. (2019). Recorded Crime – Offenders, 2017–18 *4591.0*. Canberra: Australian Bureau of Statistics.

Australian Institute of Health and Welfare. (2017). *National Drug Strategy Household Survey 2016: Detailed findings*. Drug Statistics series no. 31. Cat. no. PHE 214. Canberra: AIHW.

Bäckman, O., Estrada, F., Nilsson, A., & Shannon, D. (2014). The life course of young male and female offenders: Stability or change between different birth cohorts? *British Journal of Criminology, 54*(3), 393–410.

Becker, G. S., Landes, W. M., & National Bureau of Economic Research (eds.) (1974). *Essays in the Economics of Crime and Punishment* (Vol. 3). New York: National Bureau of Economic Research: distributed by Columbia University Press.

Berg, M. T., Baumer, E., Rosenfeld, R., & Loeber, R. (2016). Dissecting the prevalence and incidence of offending during the crime drop of the 1990s. *Journal of Quantitative Criminology, 32*(3), 377–396. doi:10.1007/s10940-016-9289-6

Bersani, B. E., Loughran, T. A., & Piquero, A. R. (2014). Comparing patterns and predictors of immigrant offending among a sample of adjudicated youth. *Journal of Youth and Adolescence, 43*(11), 1914–1933. doi:10.1007/s10964-013-0045-z

Bhati, A. S., & Piquero, A. R. (2008). Estimating the impact of incarceration on subsequent offending trajectories: Deterrent, criminogenic, or null effect? *Journal of Criminal Law & Criminology, 98*(1), 207–253.

Biderman, A. D., & Reiss, A. J. (1967). On exploring the "dark figure" of crime. *The ANNALS of the American Academy of Political and Social Science, 374* (1), 1–15. doi:10.1177/000271626737400102

Bishop, D. M. (2006). Public opinion and juvenile justice policy: Myths and misconceptions public preference for rehabilitation: Reaction essay. *Criminology and Public Policy, 5*, 653–664.

Blumstein, A. (2006). The crime drop in America: An exploration of some recent crime trends. *Journal of Scandinavian Studies in Criminology and Crime Prevention, 7*(sup1), 17–35. doi:10.1080/14043850601037938

Blumstein, A., Cohen, J., & Miller, H. D. (1980). Demographically disaggregated projections of prison populations. *Journal of Criminal Justice, 8*(1), 1–26. doi:10.1016/0047-2352(80)90056-2

Blumstein, A., & Wallman, J. (2000). *The Crime Drop in America*. New York: Cambridge University Press.

Braga, A., & Weisburd, D. (2019). Critic: Problem-oriented policing: The disconnect between principles and practice. In D. Weisburd & A. Braga (eds.), *Police Innovation: Contrasting Perspectives* (2nd ed., pp. 182–204). Cambridge, UK: Cambridge University Press.

Brown, R. (2015a). Explaining the property crime drop: The offender perspective. *Trends and Issues in Crime and Criminal Justice*, (495), 1–7.

Brown, R. (2015b). Reviewing the effectiveness of electronic vehicle immobilisation: Evidence from four countries. *Security Journal, 28*(4), 329–351. doi:10.1057/sj.2012.55

Burgess, R. L., & Akers, R. L. (1966). A differential association-reinforcement theory of criminal behavior. *Social Problems, 14*(2), 128–147.

Bursik, R. J. (1988). Social disorganization and theories of crime and delinquency: Problems and prospects. *Criminology, 26*(4), 519–552.

Canela-Cacho, J. A., Blumstein, A., & Cohen, J. (1997). Relationship between the offending frequency (lambda) of imprisoned and free offenders. *Criminology, 35*(1), 133–175. doi:10.1111/j.1745-9125.1997.tb00873.x

Caspi, A., & Moffitt, T. E. (1995). The continuity of maladaptive behavior. In D. Cicchetti & D. Cohen (eds.), *Manual of Developmental Psychopathology* (Vol. 2, pp. 472–511). New York: Wiley.

Cecil, K. M., Brubaker, C. J., Adler, C. M., et al. (2008). Decreased brain volume in adults with childhood lead exposure. *PLOS Medicine, 5*(5), e112. doi:10.1371/journal.pmed.0050112

Cecil, K. M., Dietrich, K. N., Altaye, M., Egelhoff, J. C., Lindquist, D. M., Brubaker, C. J., & Lanphear, B. P. (2011). Proton magnetic resonance spectroscopy in adults with childhood lead exposure. *Environmental Health Perspectives, 119*(3), 403–408.

Cernkovich, S. A., & Giordano, P. C. (2001). Stability and change in antisocial behavior: the transition from adolescence to early adulthood. *Criminology, 39* (2), 371–410.

Chandramouli, K., Steer, C. D., Ellis, M., & Emond, A. M. (2009). Effects of early childhood lead exposure on academic performance and behaviour of school age children. *Archives of Disease in Childhood, 94*(11), 844–848. doi:10.1136/adc.2008.149955

Clancey, G., & Lulham, R. (2014). The New South Wales property crime decline. *Current Issues in Criminal Justice, 25*(3), 839–851. doi:10.1080/ 10345329.2014.12036001

Cline, H. F. (1980). Criminal behavior over the life span. In O. G. Brim & J. Kagan (eds.), *Constancy and Change in Human Development* (pp. 641–674). Cambridge: Havard University Press.

Cloward, R. A., & Ohlin, L. E. (1960). *Delinquency and Opportunity.* New York: Free Press of Glencoe.

Cohen, L. E., & Vila, B. J. (1996). Self-control and social control: An exposition of the Gottfredson-Hirschi/Sampson Laub debate. *Studies on Crime and Crime Prevention, 5*(2), 125–150.

Cohen, M. A., & Piquero, A. R. (2009). New evidence on the monetary value of saving a high risk youth. *Journal of Quantitative Criminology, 25*(1), 25–49.

Cook, P. J., & Laub, J. H. (2002). After the epidemic: Recent trends in youth violence in the United States. *Crime and Justice, 29*, 1–37. doi:10.1086/652218

Crime Statistics Agency (CSA). (2019). Recorded Criminal Incidents. Accessed 24/01/2020: www.crimestatistics.vic.gov.au/crime-statisticslatest-crime-data/recorded-criminal-incidents-0

Cullen, F. T., Jonson, C. L., & Nagin, D. S. (2011). Prisons do not reduce recidivism: The high cost of ignoring science. *The Prison Journal, 91* (3_suppl), 48S–65S.

Degenhardt, L., Day, C., Gilmour, S., & Hall, W. (2006). The "lessons" of the Australian "heroin shortage." *Substance Abuse Treatment Prevention and Policy, 1, 11*. doi:10.1186/1747-597x-1-11

del Frate, A. A., & Mugellini, G. (2012). The crime drop in "non-western" countries: a review of homicide data. In J. van Dijk, A. Tseloni, A. & G. Farrell (eds.), *The International Crime Drop. Crime Prevention and Security Management* (pp. 134–155). London: Palgrave Macmillan.

Diamond, B., Jennings, W. G., & Piquero, A. R. (2018). Scaling-up self-control: A macro-level investigation of self-control at the county level. *Journal of Criminal Justice, 56*, 81–85. doi:10.1016/j.jcrimjus.2017.08.003

Dietrich, K. N., Douglas, R. M., Succop, P. A., Berger, O. G., & Bornschein, R. L. (2001). Early exposure to lead and juvenile delinquency. *Neurotoxicology and Teratology, 23*(6), 511–518. doi:10.1016/S0892-0362(01)00184-2

Donohue III, J. J. (2009). Assessing the relative benefits of incarceration: Overall changes and the benefits on the margin. In S. Raphael & M. Stoll (eds.), (2009). *Do prisons make us safer?: The benefits and costs of the prison boom* (pp. 269–342), Russell Sage Foundation.

Donohue, J. J., & Levitt, S. D. (2001). The impact of legalized abortion on crime. *The Quarterly Journal of Economics, 116*(2), 379–420. doi:10.1162/00335530151144050

Duell, N., Steinberg, L., Icenogle, G., et al. (2018). Age patterns in risk taking across the world. *Journal of Youth and Adolescence, 47*(5), 1052–1072. doi:10.1007/s10964-017-0752-y

Durlauf, S. N., & Nagin, D. S. (2010). The deterrent effect of imprisonment. In P. J. Cook & J. Ludwig (eds.), *Making Crime Control Pay: Cost Effective Alternatives to Incarceration*. Chicago: University of Chicago Press.

Durlauf, S. N., & Nagin, D. S. (2011). Imprisonment and crime: Can both be reduced? *Criminology & Public Policy, 10*(1), 13–54. doi:10.1111/j.1745-9133.2010.00680.x

Eck, J. E., & Madensen, T. (2009). Using signatures of opportunity structures to examine mechanisms in crime prevention evaluations. In J. Knutsson and N. Tilley (eds.), *Evaluting Crime Prevention Initiatives* (Vol. 24, pp. 59–84). Monsey, NY: Criminal Justice Press.

Eisner, M. (2014). From swords to words: Does macro-level change in self-control predict long-term variation in levels of homicide? In M. Tonry (ed.), *Crime and Justice: A Review of Research* (Vol. 43, pp. 65–134). Chicago: University of Chicago.

Ezell, M. E., & Cohen, L. E. (2005). *Desisting from Crime: Continuity and Change in Long-Term Crime Patterns of Serious Chronic Offenders*. Oxford: Oxford University Press.

Fabio, A., Loeber, R., Balasubramani, G. K., et al. (2006). Why some generations are more violent than others: Assessment of age, period, and cohort effects. *American Journal of Epidemiology, 164*(2), 151–160. doi:10.1093/aje/kwj172

Farrell, G., & Birks, D. (2018). Did cybercrime cause the crime drop? *Crime Science, 7*(1), 1–4. doi:10.1186/s40163-018-0082-8

Farrell, G., & Brantingham, P. J. (2013). The crime drop and the general social survey. *Canadian Public Policy/ Analyse De Politiques*, *39*(4), 559–580. doi:10.3138/cpp.39.4.559

Farrell, G., & Brown, R. (2016). On the origins of the crime drop: Vehicle crime and security in the 1980s. *The Howard Journal of Crime and Justice*, *55* (1–2), 226–237. doi:10.1111/hojo.12158

Farrell, G., Laycock, G., & Tilley, N. (2015). Debuts and legacies: The crime drop and the role of adolescence-limited and persistent offending. *Crime Science*, *4*(1), 1–10. doi:10.1186/s40163-015-0028-3

Farrell, G., Tilley, N., & Tseloni, A. (2014). Why the crime drop: Why crime rates fall and why they don't. *Crime and Justice: A Review of Research*, *43*, 421–490.

Farrell, G., Tilley, N., Tseloni, A., & Mailley, J. (2010). Explaining and sustaining the crime drop: Clarifying the role of opportunity-related theories. *Crime Prevention and Community Safety: An International Journal*, *12*(1), 24–41. doi:10.1057/cpcs.2009.20

Farrell, G., Tseloni, A., & Tilley, N. (2011). The effectiveness of vehicle security devices and their role in the crime drop. *Criminology & Criminal Justice*, *11*(1), 21–35. doi:10.1177/1748895810392190

Farrington, D. P., & Maughan, B. (1999). Criminal careers of two London cohorts. *Criminal Behavior and Mental Health*, *9*, 91–106. doi:10.1002/cbm.293

Farrington, D. P. (2003). Developmental and life-course criminology: Key theoretical and empirical issues – the 2002 Sutherland Award Address. *Criminology*, *41*(2), 221–256.

Farrington, D. P. (2005a). The Integrated Cognitive Antisocial Potential (ICAP) theory. In D. P. Farrington (ed.), *Integrated Developmental & Life-Course Theories of Offending* (Vol. 14, pp. 73–92). New York: Transaction Publishers.

Farrington, D. P. (2005b). Introduction to integrated developmental and life-course theories of offending. In D. P. Farrington (ed.), *Integrated Developmental & Life-Course Theories of Offending* (Vol. 14, pp. 1–14). New Jersey: Transaction Publishers.

Fox, J. A. (1978). *Forecasting Crime Data: An Econometric Analysis*. Lexington, MA: Lexington Books.

Fox, J. A. (2006). Demograghics and U.S. homicide. In A. Blumstein and J. Wallmann (eds.), *The Crime Drop in America* (Revised ed.; pp. 266–287). Cambridge: Cambridge University Press.

Gatti, U., Tremblay, R. E., & Vitaro, F. (2009). Iatrogenic effect of juvenile justice. *Journal of Child Psychology and Psychiatry*, *50*(8), 991–998. doi:10.1111/j.1469-7610.2008.02057.x

Gomez-Smith, Z., & Piquero, A. R. (2005). An examination of adult onset offending. *Journal of Criminal Justice, 33*(6), 515–525.

Gottfredson, M. R. (2005). Offender classifications and treatment effects in developmental criminology: A propensity/event consideration. *The ANNALS of the American Academy of Political and Social Science, 602* (1), 46–56.

Gottfredson, M., & Hirschi, T. (1986). The true value of lambda would appear to be zero: An essay on career criminals, criminal careers, selective incapacitation, cohort studies, and related topics. *Criminology, 24*(2), 213–234.

Gottfredson, M. R., & Hirschi, T. (1990). *A General Theory of Crime.* Stanford, CA: Stanford University Press.

Gove, W. R. (1985). The effect of age and gender on deviant behavior: A biopsychosocial perspective. In A. Rossi (ed.), *Gender and the Life Course* (pp. 115–144). New York: Aldine De Gruyter.

Grogger, J. (2006). An economic model of recent trends in violence. In A. Blumstein and J. Wallman (eds.), *The Crime Drop in America* (revised ed., pp. 266–287). Cambridge: Cambridge University Press.

Grucza, R. A., Sher, K. J., Kerr, W. C., et al. (2018). Trends in adult alcohol use and binge drinking in the early 21st-century United States: A meta-analysis of 6 national survey series. *Alcohol Clin Exp Res, 42*(10), 1939–1950. doi:10.1111/acer.13859

Hanslmaier, M., Kemme, S., Stoll, K., & Baier, D. (2015). Forecasting crime in Germany in times of demographic change. *European Journal on Criminal Policy and Research, 21*(4), 591–610. doi:10.1007/s10610-015-9270-1

Hirschi, T. (1986). On the compatibility of rational choice and social control theories of crime. In D. Cornish & R. Clarke (eds.), *The Reasoning Criminal: Rational Choice Perspectives on Offending* (pp. 105–118). Secaucus: Springer-Verlag.

Hirschi, T. (1998). Social bond theory. In F. Cullen & R. Agnew (eds.), *Criminological Theory: Past to Present* (pp. 167–174). Los Angeles: Roxbury.

Hirschi, T., & Gottfredson, M. R. (1983). Age and the explanation of crime. *American Journal of Sociology, 89*(3), 552–584.

Hodgkinson, T., Andresen, M. A., & Farrell, G. (2016). The decline and locational shift of automotive theft: A local level analysis. *Journal of Criminal Justice, 44*, 49–57. doi:10.1016/j.jcrimjus.2015.12.003

Hua, J., Baker, J., & Poynton, S. (2006). Generation Y and Crime: A longitudinal study of contact with NSW criminal courts before the age of 21 *Contemporary Issues in Criminal Justice.* Sydney: NSW Beureau of Crime Statistcs and Research.

Ignatans, D., & Matthews, R. (2017). Immigration and the crime drop. *European Journal of Crime, Criminal Law and Criminal Justice, 25*(3), 205–229. doi:10.1163/15718174-02503002

Jennings, W. G., Loeber, R., Pardini, D., Piquero, A. R., & Farrington, D. P. (2016). *Offending from Childhood to Young Adulthood: Recent Results from the Pittsburgh Youth Study.* New York: Springer.

Jennings, W. G., & Reingle, J. M. (2012). On the number and shape of developmental/life-course violence, aggression, and delinquency trajectories: A state-of-the-art review. *Journal of Criminal Justice, 40*(6), 472–489. doi:10.1016/j.jcrimjus.2012.07.001

Johnson, B., Golub, A., & Dunlap, E. (2000). The rise and decline of hard drugs, drug markets, and violence in inner-city New York. In A. Blumstein and J Wallman (eds.), *The crime drop in America* (pp. 164–206). Cambridge: Cambridge University Press.

Jones, B. L., & Nagin, D. S. (2013). A note on a Stata plugin for estimating group-based trajectory models. *Sociological Methods & Research, 42*(4), 608–613.

Kim, J., Bushway, S., Tsao, H.-S. (2015). Identifying classes of explanations for crime drop: Period and cohort effects for New York State. *Journal of Quantitative Criminology, 32*(3), 357–375.

Kim, J., Bushway, S., & Tsao, H.-S. (2016). Identifying classes of explanations for crime drop: period and cohort effects for New York State. *Journal of Quantitative Criminology, 32*(3), 357–375. doi: http://dx.doi.org/10.1007 /s10940-015-9274-5

Kovandzic, T. V., Schaffer, M. E., Vieraitis, L. M., Orrick, E. A., & Piquero, A. R. (2016). Police, crime and the problem of weak instruments: Revisiting the "More Police, Less Crime" thesis. *Journal of Quantitative Criminology, 32*(1), 133–158. doi:10.1007/s10940-015-9257-6

Kriven, S., & Ziersch, E. (2007). New car security and shifting vehicle theft patterns in Australia. *Security Journal, 20*(2), 111–122. doi:10.1057/palgrave.sj.8350026

Krohn, M. D., Gibson, C. L., & Thornberry, T. P. (2013). Under the protective bud the bloom awaits: A review of theory and research on adult-onset and late-blooming offenders. In C. L. Gibson & M. D. Krohn (eds.), *Handbook of Life-Course Criminology: Emerging Trends and Directions for Future Research* (pp. 183–200). New York: Springer.

Laub, J. H. (2004). The life course of criminology in the United States: The American Society of Criminology 2003 presidential address. *Criminology, 42*(1), 1–26. doi:10.1111/j.1745-9125.2004.tb00511.x

Levitt, S. D. (1999). The limited role of changing age strucutre in explaining aggregate crime rates. *Criminology, 37*(3), 581–598. doi:10.1111/j.1745-9125.1999.tb00497.x

Levitt, S. D. (2004). Understanding why crime fell in the 1990s: Four factors that explain the decline and six that do not. *The Journal of Economic Perspectives, 18*(1), 163–190. doi:10.1257/089533004773563485

Liedka, R. V., Piehl, A. M., & Useem, B. (2006). The crime-control effect of incarceration: Does scale matter? *Criminology & Public Policy, 5*(2), 245–276. doi:10.1111/j.1745-9133.2006.00376.x

Livingston, M., Raninen, J., Slade, T., Swift, W., Lloyd, B., & Dietze, P. (2016). Understanding trends in Australian alcohol consumption—an age–period–cohort model. *Addiction, 111*(9), 1590–1598.

Loeber, R., & Farrington, D. P. (2014). Age-crime curve. In *Encyclopedia of Criminology and Criminal Justice* (pp. 12–18). New York: Springer.

Loeber, R., Jennings, W., Ahonen, L., Piquero, A. R., & Farrington, D. P. (2017). *Female Delinquency from Childhood to Young Adulthood: Recent Results from the Pittsburgh Youth Study.* New York: Springer.

Loeber, R., & Le Blanc, M. (1990). Toward a developmental criminology. In M. Tonry & N. Morris (eds.), *Crime and Justice* (Vol. 12, pp. 375–473). Chicago: University of Chicago Press.

Markowitz, F. E., Bellair, P. E., Liska, A. E., & Liu, J. (2001). Extending social disorganization theory: Modeling the relationships between cohesion, disorder, and fear. *Criminology, 39*(2), 293–319.

Marvell, T. B., & Moody, C. E. (1994). Prison population growth and crime reduction. *Journal of Quantitative Criminology, 10*(2), 109–140. doi:10.1007/BF02221155

Matsueda, R. L. (1988). The current state of differential association theory. *Crime & Delinquency, 34*(3), 277–306.

Matsueda, R. L. (2001). Differential association theory. In C. D. Bryant (ed.), *Encyclopedia of Criminology and Deviant Behavior* (Vol. 1, pp. 125–130). New York: Taylor and Francis.

Matthews, B., & Minton, J. (2018). Rethinking one of criminology's "brute facts": The age–crime curve and the crime drop in Scotland. *European Journal of Criminology, 15*(3), 296–320. doi:10.1177/1477370817731706

Mayhew, P. (2012). The case of Australia and New Zealand. In J. van Dijk, A. Tseloni & G. Farrell (eds.), *The International Crime Drop: Crime Prevention and Security Management.* London: Palgrave Macmillan

McCord, J. (1980). Patterns of deviance. In S. B. Sells, R. Crandall, M. Roff, J. S. Strauss & W. Pollin (eds.), *Human Functioning in Longitudinal Perspective* (pp. 157–162). Baltimore: Williams and Walkins.

Merton, R. K. (1938). Social structure and anomie. *American Sociological Review*, 3(5), 672–682.

Mishra, S., & Lalumière, M. (2009). Is the crime drop of the 1990s in Canada and the USA associated with a general decline in risky and health-related behavior? *Social Science & Medicine*, 68(1), 39–48. doi:https://doi.org/10.1016/j.socscimed.2008.09.060

MM Starrs, Ltd. (2002). *Principles for Compulsory Immobiliser Schemes*. Melbourne.

Moffatt, S., Weatherburn, D., & Donnelly, N. (2005). *What Caused the Recent Drop in Property Crime?* Sydney: NSW Bureau of Crime Statistics and Research.

Moffitt, T. E. (1993). Life-course-persistent and adolescence-limited antisocial behavior: A developmental taxonomy. *Psychological Review, 100.4*, 674–701.

Moffitt, T. E. (1997). Adolescence-limited and life-course persistent offending: A complimentary pair of developmental theories. In T. P. Thornberry (ed.), *Developmental Theories of Crime and Delinquency* (Vol. 7, pp. 11–54). New York: Transaction Publishers.

Moffitt, T. E. (2003). Life-course-persistent and adolescence-limited antisocial behavior: A 10-year research review and a research agenda. In B. B. Lahey, T. E. Moffitt, & A. Caspi (Eds.), *Causes of Conduct Disorder and Juvenile Delinquency* (pp. 49–75). New York: The Guilford Press.

Moffitt, T. E., & Caspi, A. (2001). Childhood predictors differentiate life-course persistent and adolescence-limited antisocial pathways among males and females. *Development and Psychopathology*, 13(2), 355–375.

Monahan, K., Steinberg, L., & Piquero, A. R. (2015). Juvenile justice policy and practice: A developmental perspective. *Crime and Justice*, 44(1), 577–619.

Morgan, N. (2014). *The Heroin Epidemic of the 1980s and 1990s and Its Effect on Crime Trends – Then and Now: Technical Report*. London: Home Office.

Nagin, D. S., Farrington, D. P., & Pogarsky, G. (1997). Adolescent mothers and the criminal behavior of their children. *Law & Society Review*, 31, 137–162.

Nagin, D. S., & Land, K. C. (1993). Age, criminal careers, and population heterogeneity: Specification and estimation of a nonparametric, mixed Poisson model. *Criminology*, 31(3), 327–362.

Nagin, D. S., & Paternoster, R. (2000). Population heterogeneity and state dependence: State of the evidence and directions for future research. *Journal of Quantitative Criminology*, 16(2), 117–144. doi:10.1023/A:1007502804941

Nagin, D. S., Piquero, A. R., Scott, E. S., & Steinberg, L. (2006). Public preferences for rehabilitation versus incarceration of juvenile offenders: Evidence from a contingent valuation survey. *Criminology & Public Policy*, 5(4), 627–651.

Nagin, D. S., Solow, R. M., & Lum, C. (2015). Deterrence, criminal opportunities, and police. *Criminology, 53*(1), 74–100. doi:10.1111/1745-9125.12057

National Academy of Sciences, Engineering and Medicine. (2016). *Modernizing Crime Statistics: Report 1: Defining and Classifying Crime.* Washington, DC.

National Academies of Sciences, Engineering and Medicine. (2018). *Proactive Policing: Effects on Crime and Communities.* National Academies Press.

National Motor Vehicle Theft Reduction Council (NMVTRC). (2007). The effectiveness of immobilisers in preventing vehicle theft in Australia. *CARS Brief Report, April 2007.*

Needleman, H. L., Schell, A., Bellinger, D., Leviton, A., & Allred, E. N. (1990). The long-term effects of exposure to low doses of lead in childhood. *New England Journal of Medicine, 322*(2), 83–88. doi:10.1056/NEJM199001113220203

Norström, T., & Svensson, J. (2014). No polarization in youth drinking in Stockholm county: response to Hallgren. *Addiction, 109*(8), 1385–1386.

NSW Bureau of Crime Statistics and Research (BOCSAR). (2019). New South Wales Recorded Crime Statistics: Quarterly Update (September 2019) *Statistical Report Series.* Sydney: NSW Bureau of Crime Statistics and Research.

Olds, D., Henderson, J., Charles R., et al. (1998). Long-term effects of nurse home visitation on children's criminal and antisocial behavior: 15-year follow-up of a randomized controlled trial. *JAMA, 280*(14), 1238–1244. doi:10.1001/jama.280.14.1238

Orrick, E. A., & Piquero, A. R. (2015). Were cell phones associated with lower crime in the 1990s and 2000s? *Journal of Crime & Justice, 38*(2), 222–234. doi:10.1080/0735648x.2013.864570

Ouimet, M. (1999). Crime in Canada and in the United States: A comparative analysis. *Canadian Review of Sociology and Anthropology-Revue Canadienne De Sociologie Et D Anthropologie, 36*(3), 389–408. doi:10.1111/j.1755-618X.1999.tb00581.x

Ouimet, M. (2002). Explaining the American and Canadian crime "drop" in the 1990's. *Canadian Journal of Criminology-Revue Canadienne De Criminologie, 44*(1), 33–50.

Ousey, G. C., & Kubrin, C. E. (2009). Exploring the Connection between immigration and violent crime rates in U.S. Cities, 1980–2000. *Social Problems, 56*(3), 447–473. doi:10.1525/sp.2009.56.3.447

Paternoster, R., Dean, C. W., Piquero, A., Mazerolle, P., & Brame, R. (1997). Generality, continuity, and change in offending. *Journal of Quantitative Criminology, 13*(3), 231–266. doi:10.1007/bf02221092

Payne, J. L., & Piquero, A. R. (2016). The concordance of self-reported and officially recorded lifetime offending histories: Results from a sample of

Australian prisoners. *Journal of Criminal Justice, 46*, 184–195. doi:10.1016/j.jcrimjus.2016.05.004

Payne, J., Brown, R., & Broadhurst, R. (2016). Dataset: Trajectories of two NSW Birth Cohorts. *Data supplied by the NSW Bureau of Crime Statistics and Research*. Research funded by the Criminology Research Council.

Payne J., Brown R., & Broadhurst R., (2018). Where have all the young offenders gone? Examining changes in offending between two NSW birth cohorts. *Trends & issues in crime and criminal justice* no. 553. Canberra: Australian Institute of Criminology.

Payne J., Kwiatkowski M. & Wundersitz J. (2008). *Police Drug Diversion: A Study of Criminal Offending Outcomes*. Research and Public Policy Series No. 97. Canberra: Australian Institute of Criminology. https://aic.gov.au/publications/rpp/rpp97

Piquero, A. R. (2008). Disproportionate minority contact. *Future of Children, 18*(2), 59–79. doi:10.1353/foc.0.0013

Piquero, A. R., & Blumstein, A. (2007). Does incapacitation reduce crime? *Journal of Quantitative Criminology, 23*(4), 267–285. doi:10.1007/s10940-007-9030-6

Piquero, A. R., Brame, R., & Moffitt, T. E. (2005). Extending the study of continuity and change: Gender differences in the linkage between adolescent and adult offending. *Journal of Quantitative Criminology, 21*(2), 219–243. doi:10.1007/s10940-005-2494-3

Piquero, A. R., Farrington, D. P., & Blumstein, A. (2003). The criminal career paradigm: background and recent developments. *Crime and justice, 30*, 359–506.

Piquero, A. R., Jennings, W. G., & Farrington, D. P. (2010). On the malleability of self-control: Theoretical and policy implications regarding a general theory of crime. *Justice Quarterly, 27*(6), 803–834. doi:10.1080/07418820903379628

Piquero, A. R., Piquero, N. L., & Narvey, C. (2019). Developmental and life course perspectives on female offending. In L. B. Shelley & L. Gelsthorpe (eds.), *The Wiley Handbook on What Works with Female Offenders: A Critical Review of Theory, Practice, and Policy*: Hoboken, New Jersey.

Piquero, A. R., Farrington, D. P., Welsh, B. C., Tremblay, R., & Jennings, W. G. (2009). Effects of early family/parent training programs on antisocial behavior and delinquency. *Journal of Experimental Criminology, 5*, 83–120.

Piquero, A. R., Jennings, W. G., Diamond, B., Farrington, D. P., Tremblay, R. E., Welsh, B. C., & Gonzalez, J. M. R. (2016). A meta-analysis update on the effects of early family/parent training programs on antisocial behavior and delinquency. *Journal of Experimental Criminology, 12*(2), 229–248.

Piquero, N. L., & Piquero, A. R. (2015). Life-course-persistent offending. In F. T. Cullen, P. Wilcox, J. L. Lux, & C. L. Jonson (eds.), *Sisters in Crime Revisited: Bringing Gender into Criminology*. New York: Oxford University Press.

Potter, R., & Thomas, P. (2001). *Engine immobilisers: how effective are they?* National Motor Vehicle Theft Reduction Council. Last accessed May 2020. https://carsafe.com.au/docs/immobiliser_paper.pdf.

Quetelet, A. (2003 [1831]). Research on the propensity for crime at different ages. Translated by Sylveski, S. F. In P. Bean (ed.), *Crime: Critical Concepts in Sociology* (pp. 119–135). London: Taylor & Francis.

Radaev, V., & Roshchina, Y. (2019). Young cohorts of Russians drink less: age–period–cohort modelling of alcohol use prevalence 1994–2016. *Addiction*, *114*(5), 823–835.

Raninen, J., Livingston, M., & Leifman, H. (2014). Declining trends in alcohol consumption among Swedish youth—does the theory of collectivity of drinking cultures apply?. *Alcohol and Alcoholism*, *49*(6), 681–686.

Raphael, S., & Winter-Ebmer, R. (2001). Identifying the effect of unemployment on crime. *The Journal of Law & Economics*, *44*(1), 259–283. doi:10.1086/320275

Reyes, J. W. (2007). Environmental policy as social policy? The impact of childhood lead exposure on crime. *The B.E. Journal of Economic Analysis & Policy*, *7*(1), 51. doi:10.2202/1935-1682.1796

Robins, L. N. (1978). Sturdy childhood predictors of adult antisocial behavior: Replications from longitudinal studies. *Psychological medicine*, *8*(4), 611–622.

Robins, L. N., & Rutter, M. (1990). *Straight and Devious Pathways from Childhood to Adulthood*. Cambridge: Cambridge University Press.

Roeder, O. K., Eisen, L.-B., Bowling, J., Stiglitz, J. E., & Chettiar, I. M. (2015). What caused crime to decline? Columbia Business School Research Paper (Vol. 15–28). Columbia: Columbia University.

Rosenfeld, R., & Messner, S. F. (1995). Crime and the American dream: An institutional analysis. In F. Adler & W. Laufer (eds.), *The Legacy of Anomie Theory* (pp. 159–182). New Jersey: Transation.

Rutter, M., Quinton, D., & Hill, J. (1990). Adult outcome of institution-reared children: Males and females compared. In L. N. Robins & M. Rutter (eds.), *Straight and Devious Pathways from Childhood to Adulthood* (pp. 135–157). Cambridge: Cambridge University Press.

Sampson, J. R. (2000). Whither the sociological study of crime? *Annual Review of Sociology*, *26*, 711–714.

Sampson, J. R., & Groves, W. B. (1989). Community structure and crime: Testing social-disorganization theory. *American Journal of Sociology*, *94*(4), 774–802.

Sampson, J. R., & Laub, J. H. (1997). A life-course theory of cumulative disadvantage and stability in delinquency. In T. P. Thornberry (ed.), *Developmental Theories of Crime and Delinquency* (Vol. 7, pp. 133–162). New Jersey: Transaction Publishers.

Sampson, J. R., & Laub, J. H. (2003a). Life-course desisters? Trajectories of crime among delinquent boys followed to age 70. *Criminology, 41*(3), 555–592.

Sampson, J. R., & Laub, J. H. (2003b). *Shared Beginnings, Divergent Lives: Delinquent Boys to Age 70*. Canbridge: Harvard University Press.

Sampson, R. J., & Lydia, B. (2006). "Cultural Mechanisms and Killing Fields: A Revised Theory of Community-Level Racial Inequality." *The Many Colors of Crime: Inequalities of Race, Ethnicity and Crime in America*, edited by Ruth Peterson, Lauren Krivo, and John Hagan. New York: New York University Press.

Sampson, R. J., & Laub, J. H. (1993). Turning points in the life course: Why change matters to the study of crime. *Criminology, 31*(3), 301–325. doi:10.1111/j.1745-9125.1993.tb01132.x

Sanders, T., Liu, Y., Buchner, V., & Tchounwou, P. B. (2009). Neurotoxic effects and biomarkers of lead exposure: a review. *Reviews on Environmental Health, 24*(1), 15–46.

Sherman, L. W. (1995). Police. In J. Q. Wilson & J. Petersilia (eds.), *Crime*. San Francisco: ICS Press.

Sherman, L. W., Gartin, P. R., & Buerger, M. E. (1989). Hot spots of predatory crime: Routine activities and the criminology of place. *Criminology, 27*(1), 27–56. doi:10.1111/j.1745-9125.1989.tb00862.x

Shoesmith, G. L. (2017). Crime, teenage abortion, and unwantedness. *Crime & Delinquency, 63*(11), 1458–1490. doi:10.1177/0011128715615882

Sidebottom, A., Kuo, T., Mori, T., Li, J., & Farrell, G. (2018). The East Asian crime drop?. *Crime Science, 7*(1), 1–6.

Soothill, K., Ackerley, E., & Francis, B. (2008). Criminal convictions among children and young adults: Changes over time. *Criminology & Criminal Justice, 8*(3), 297–315. doi:10.1177/1748895808092431

Spelman, W. (1994). *Criminal Incapacitation*. New York: Plenum Press.

Spelman, W. (2000). What recent studies do (and don't) tell us about imprisonment and crime. *Crime and Justice, 27*, 419–494. doi:10.1086/652204

Stowell, J. I., Messner, S. F., McGeever, K. F., & Raffalovich, L. E. (2009). Immigration and the recent violent crime drop in the United States: A pooled, cross-sectional time-series analysis of metropolitan areas. *Criminology, 47* (3), 889–928. doi:10.1111/j.1745-9125.2009.00162.x

Telep, C. W., & Weisburd, D. (2012). What is known about the effectiveness of police practices in reducing crime and disorder? *Police Quarterly, 15*(4), 331–357. doi:10.1177/1098611112447611

Törrönen, J., Roumeliotis, F., Samuelsson, E., Kraus, L., & Room, R. (2019). Why are young people drinking less than earlier? Identifying and specifying social mechanisms with a pragmatist approach. *International Journal of Drug Policy, 64*, 13–20.

Tracy, P., & Kempf-Leonard, K. (1996). *Continuity and Discontinuity in Criminal Careers.* New York: Plenum Press.

Tracy, P., Wolfgang, M. E., & Figlio, R. M. (1990). *Delinquency Careers in Two Birth Cohorts*: Plenum Press, New York.

Trussler, T. (2012). Demographics and homicide in Canada: A fixed-effects analysis of the role of young males on changing homicide rates. *Western Criminology Review, 13*(1), 53–67.

Tseloni, A., Thompson, R., Grove, L., Tilley, N., & Farrell, G. (2017). The effectiveness of burglary security devices. *Security Journal, 30*(2), 646–664. doi:10.1057/sj.2014.30

van Dijk, J., Mayhew, P., & Killias, M. (1990). *Experiences of Crime across the World: Key Findings from the 1989 International Crime Survey.* Deventer: Kluwer Law and Taxation.

van Dijk, J., & Tseloni, A. (2012). Global overview: International trends in victimization and recorded crime. In J. van Dijk, A. Tseloni & G. Farrell (eds.), *The International Crime Drop: New Directions in Research* (pp. 11–36). London: Palgrave Macmillan UK.

van Dijk, J., & Vollaard, B. (2012). Self-limiting crime waves. In J. van Dijk, A. Tseloni & G. Farrell (eds.), *The International Crime Drop: New Directions in Research* (pp. 250–267). London: Palgrave Macmillan.

van Vugt, E., Loeber, R., & Pardini, D. (2016). Why is young maternal age at first childbirth a risk factor for persistent delinquency in their male offspring? Examining the role of family and parenting factors. *Criminal Behaviour and Mental Health, 26*(5), 322–335. doi:10.1002/cbm.1959

Vlasak, T., Jordakieva, G., Gnambs, T., Augner, C., Crevenna, R., Winker, R., & Barth, A. (2019). Blood lead levels and cognitive functioning: A meta-analysis. *Science of The Total Environment, 668*, 678–684. doi:https://doi.org/10.1016/j.scitotenv.2019.03.052

von Hofer, H. (2014). Crime and reactions to crime in 34 Swedish birth cohorts: From historical descriptions to forecasting the future. *Journal of Scandinavian Studies in Criminology and Crime Prevention, 15*(2), 167–181. doi:10.1080/14043858.2014.918298

Wadsworth, T. (2010). Is immigration responsible for the crime drop? An assessment of the influence of immigration on changes in violent crime between 1990 and 2000. *Social Science Quarterly, 91*(2), 531–553. doi:10.1111/j.1540-6237.2010.00706.x

Wan, W.-Y., Moffatt, S., Jones, C., & Weatherburn, D. (2012). The effect of arrest and imprisonment on crime. *Crime And Justice Bulletin*, No.158. Sydney: NSW Bureau of Crime Statistics and Research.

Weatherburn, D. (2014). *Arresting Incarceration: Pathways out of Indigenous Imprisonment.* Canberra: Aboriginal Studies Press.

Weatherburn, D., Freeman, K., & Holmes, J. (2014). Young but not so restless: Trends in the age-specific rate of offending. *Crime and Justice Statistics.* (Issue Paper No. 98) Sydney: NSW Bureau of Crime Statistics and Research.

Weatherburn, D., Halstead, I., & Ramsey, S. (2016). The great (Australian) property crime decline. *Australian Journal of Social Issues*, *51*(3), 257–278. doi:10.1002/j.1839-4655.2016.tb01231.x

Weatherburn, D., & Holmes, J. (2013). *The Decline in Robbery and Theft: Interstate Comparisons.* Sydney: NSW Bureau of Crime Statistics and Research.

Weatherburn, D., Jones, C., Freeman, K., & Makkai, T. (2003). Supply control and harm reduction: Lessons from the Australian heroin "drought." *Addiction*, *98*(1), 83–91. doi:10.1046/j.1360-0443.2003.00248.x

Weisburd, D. (2018). Hot spots of crime and place-based prevention. *Criminology & Public Policy*, *17*(1), 5–25. doi:10.1111/1745-9133.12350

Weisburd, D., Bushway, S., Lum, C., & Yang, S.-M. (2004). Trajectories of crime at places: A longitudinal study of street segments in the City of Seattle. *Criminology*, *42*(2), 283–322.

Weisburd, D., Mastrofski, S. D., Willis, J. J., & Greenspan, R. (2019). Changing everything so that everything can remain the same: Compstat and American policing. In D. Weisburd & A. Braga (eds.), *Police Innovation: Contrasting Perspectives* (2nd ed., pp. 417–438). Cambridge: Cambridge University Press.

Winter, A. S., & Sampson, R. J. (2017). From lead exposure in early childhood to adolescent health: A Chicago birth cohort. *American Journal of Public Health*, *107*(9), 1496–1501. doi:10.2105/ajph.2017.303903

Wolfgang, M. E., Figlio, R. M., & Sellin, T. (1972). *Delinquency in a Birth Cohort.* Chicago: University of Chicago Press.

Wright, J. P., Dietrich, K. N., Ris, M. D., et al. (2008). Association of prenatal and childhood blood lead concentrations with criminal arrests in early adulthood. *PLOS Medicine*, *5*(5), e101. doi:10.1371/journal.pmed.0050101

Zara, G., & Farrington, D. P. (2009). Childhood and adolescent predictors of late onset criminal careers. *Journal of Youth and Adolescence*, *38*(3), 287–300.

Zimring, F. E. (2007). *The Great American Crime Decline.* New York: Oxford University Press.

Zimring, F. E. (2012). *The City That Became Safe: New York's Lessons for Urban Crime and Its Control.* New York: Cambridge University Press.

Acknowledgments

This Element uses data collected under a grant from the Australian Criminology Research Advisory Council (CRAC). The authors wish to acknowledge the kind support of the Australian Institute of Criminology (AIC) and the data extraction efforts of the NSW Bureau of Crime Statistics and Research (BOCSAR) and the NSW Registry of Births Deaths and Marriages. We also wish to extend a special acknowledgment to Dr. Rick Brown and Professor Roderic Broadhurst for their early contribution and support to the initial CRAC-funded research project.

About the Authors

Jason L. Payne is Associate Professor of Criminology in the Centre for Social Research and Methods at the Australian National University. He was formerly a research manager at the Australian Institute of Criminology, where he coordinated the National Homicide Monitoring Program, the National Deaths in Custody Program and the Drug Use Monitoring in Australia Program. His research interests include criminal careers, drug use, and recidivism and offender programs. He has evaluated a number of national and jurisdictional drug diversion and drug court programs and has received the prestigious Australian Award for University Teaching (Early Career). Jason represents the Australian Capital Territory (ACT) on the Australian and New Zealand Society of Criminology (ANZSOC) Committee of Management.

Alex R. Piquero is Professor and Chair of the Department of Sociology and Arts & Sciences Distinguished Scholar at The University of Miami and Professor of Criminology at Monash University in Melbourne Australia. He is also editor of *Justice Evaluation Journal*. His research interests include criminal careers, criminological theory, crime policy, evidence-based crime prevention, and quantitative research methods. He has received several research, teaching, and service awards and is fellow of both the American Society of Criminology and the Academy of Criminal Justice Sciences. He has received several research, teaching, and mentoring awards and in 2019, he received the Academy of Criminal Justice Sciences Bruce Smith, Sr. Award for outstanding contributions to criminal justice.

About the Series
Elements in Criminology seeks to identify key contributions in theory and empirical research that help to stake out advances in contemporary criminology. Rather than summarizing traditional theories and approaches, *Elements in Criminology* seeks to advance "turning points" in recent years, and to identify new turning points as they emerge. The series seeks a mix of forward-looking analytical reviews, as well as reports on innovative new research.

Printed in the United States
By Bookmasters